Miranda Tapsell was born in Darwin and her people are the Larrakia. After finishing school, she was accepted to study at NIDA fulltime and since graduating has built a stellar career on stage, screen and television. After a starring role in the world-renowned film *The Sapphires*, Miranda received two Logie Awards for her role in *Love Child*. A career highlight saw Miranda cast as the new host of the perennial favourite children's series, *Play School*. Recently, she has had roles on Channel 9's *Doctor Doctor* and the ABC's comedy *Get Krack!n*.

Miranda wrote, produced and starred in the box office hit *Top End Wedding* and has her own podcast on BuzzFeed, *Pretty for an Aboriginal*, with Nakkiah Lui, which rocks the traditional perceptions of Indigenous Australia and challenges rigid mindsets of what women of colour can and cannot do. *Top End Girl* is her first book.

TOP END GIRL

TOP END GIRL

MIRANDA TAPSELL

hachette
AUSTRALIA

Author's note: While this is a mostly uplifting book about my very charmed life, it is important to me that readers know that you might learn some things that are confronting and upsetting. In my life I have always taken the good with the bad. I'd also like to warn Aboriginal and Torres Strait Islander readers that there is reference to and images of people who have passed away. If anything you read distresses you, please reach out for help. There are some contact details at the back of the book that could assist you.

Love,
Miranda

hachette
AUSTRALIA

Published in Australia and New Zealand in 2020
by Hachette Australia
(an imprint of Hachette Australia Pty Limited)
Level 17, 207 Kent Street, Sydney NSW 2000
www.hachette.com.au

A catalogue record for this book is available from the National Library of Australia

ISBN: 978 0 7336 4243 2 (paperback)

Cover and internal picture section design by Christabella Designs
Cover photograph courtesy of Jason Ierace
Back cover photographs courtesy of the author; John Platt, Goalpost Pictures; and Amelia J Dowd
Typeset in Adobe Garamond Pro by Kirby Jones
Printed and bound in Australia by McPherson's Printing Group

MIX
Paper from
responsible sources
FSC
www.fsc.org   FSC® C001695

The paper this book is printed on is certified against the Forest Stewardship Council® Standards. McPherson's Printing Group holds FSC® chain of custody certification SA-COC-005379. FSC® promotes environmentally responsible, socially beneficial and economically viable management of the world's forests.

I wish to dedicate this book to my family.

This book is also for the loved ones I've had to say
goodbye to before they had a chance to see the woman
I have become. It's because of their love and support
that all my hard work paid off. I am thankful for the impact
each one had on me and I miss them terribly.

CONTENTS

IF YOU LEAVE ME NOW ... YOU'LL MISS IT ALL

HELLO.

Who the hell co-writes, produces and acts in a film about a wedding in the same year they're having their own wedding? Well ... me.

One of my best friends, Alicia, who was going to be one of my bridesmaids, once said to me, 'Miranda, you always pick the hardest path.' We've known each other since we were five, so sometimes I have to admit she knows me better than I know myself.

Alicia and I met on the first day of year one at the school in Jabiru, a small mining town in Kakadu National Park up in the Northern Territory. When I found out we were both the newbies of the class, I immediately proclaimed we were best friends. I know, it's terrible that I forced her to be my friend back then and all these years later my bridesmaid. I'm a monster.

But she is right. And now I am also writing a book about this crazy year, among other things. I never thought I'd write a film, let alone a book. So, I do make things challenging for myself. Inspirational memes often make me roll my eyes but I saw one on social media that said, 'Good things happen to babes who hustle.' Turns out I'm one hundred per cent that babe. The one who hustles constantly. Look at me trying to make things happen. A wedding. A film about a wedding. Now a book about a film about a wedding. I am very flattered if you have these pages in your hot little hands. Major brownie points go to you if you actually bought it. If someone has lent you the book and told you, '*You have to read this!*' then they also rule.

I'm very touched when I meet people who have followed my career as an actor. I put my heart and soul into what I do, so it's touching when I learn how much enjoyment people have gotten from my work—but it's also humbling to be reminded that my acting career isn't the centre of everyone's universe.

'You look familiar,' is something I hear often, and people sometimes ask, 'Have we met before? Have I seen you in something?'

When strangers figure out I'm not just the girl they knew from school but someone with a profile, they often beg me to tell them what they've seen me in. I give them a cheeky smile and say, 'It'll come back to you.' I kind of like leaving them hanging and I don't want to blow my own trumpet. It can be a shock to the old ego if someone asks for a photo with you after realising they haven't watched anything you've done. But that's all part of the hustle, baby.

I think the most embarrassing experience was when I finally decided to jog someone's memory. A woman working in an opportunity store had asked me where she'd seen me before, and I admitted I was in a film called *The Sapphires*. She replied with a very levelling, 'Oh right-o, I didn't mean that—I thought you'd served me at Coles. So, you're an actor, ay? That must be fun.'

Listen, I'm not saying there's anything wrong with working at a supermarket. And the woman must have had a really compelling conversation with the actual person who served her at the checkout. I wonder what they covered in the short time her groceries were being scanned? It was obviously memorable. The truth is, I'm living my dream and even when I am mistaken for an old school friend or the checkout chick, I am thrilled that somehow my face has registered with them.

I love what I do and the life I am living. And it is not only my career that is giving me that sense of joy. I have also been living my own real-life rom-com. I am going to tell you all about that (and a man named James) as well. Sharing my story is important. I haven't always been confident enough to hold my space in life or on the stage; to believe I could write a film, produce a film, step out from behind a role and risk making mistakes to hold the door open for others behind me, just as actors such as Aaron Pedersen, Deborah Mailman and Leah Purcell forged a path I could follow. I think it is true that you don't aspire to be what you cannot see. I would like this book to show that you can push yourself to do things you never dreamed you would do. For that shy young woman who doesn't fit the typical casting beliefs to put her talent on the line and make casting directors change their mind. For writers and producers and filmmakers to see the real place we now call Australia and the people who make up that picture. For this book to inspire others to chase what they want and to stay true to themselves in the process.

I have moments in my life that have challenged me, where others have tried to define me because of where I am from, the colour of my skin, my values, my gender and my physical appearance. Growing up, it was performing that made me feel really empowered. Knowing what I wanted out of my life, even if it was working in an industry full of uncertainty, I had a new appreciation of who I saw in the mirror. This new sense of purpose became a form of armour as I stepped into the adult world. It began to bother me less if people implied, even if they were joking, that me being short, Aboriginal and female was some kind of a detriment to who I was. While this in no way changes the way policy or law continue to affect Aboriginal and Torres Strait Islanders, I finally had a reason to get out of bed. It was a good start. I realised after drama school that staying true to the essence of what makes you unique is how people can end up casting you. While I can't change bigger social issues as an actor, I found that performing was a way of subverting the negative perceptions people had placed on people like me. It's no small thing that women, particularly young Aboriginal and Torres Strait Islander women, have felt validated because of seeing someone who looks, thinks and feels the way they do.

My parents always encouraged me to stay true to who I am, and to hold fast to the fact that being Aboriginal is something to be proud of.

And so, to all those young Black kids reading this who think they don't fit, who are made to feel ashamed of who they inherently are, please know that this Aboriginal woman has been where you are, and I know how far you can go. Believe in yourself.

So, settle in and let's begin. No refunds!

CHAPTER ONE

NOT A SUGAR PLUM

Ever since I was thirteen years old all I wanted to do was perform. It was an unusual dream for a kid from the Northern Territory to have. It's not that people didn't have hopes or aspirations where I grew up, it's just that what I wanted for my life was a world away from what people knew and loved about the 'Top End'.

Many Australians visualise Darwin and the Top End in the way Americans might describe the 'Deep South' in the United States—that it's hot, full of ignorant rednecks, absolutely nothing happens there and our biggest claim to fame is the fact we have the alligator's cousin, the crocodile, roaming our streets. That isn't the case but the local paper, the *NT News*, doesn't help debunk the myth. For those who haven't read anything from the *NT News*, the front page often boasts headlines like—'Why I Stuck a Cracker Up My Clacker', 'They Stole My Dog While I Was on the Bog', 'Horny Ghost Haunts House' and my personal favourite: 'Best Man Left Bleeding After Being Hit in the Head with Flying Dildo'. Yes, the paper can exist in a bubble from the rest of the world and I'd be lying if I said that element of the NT wasn't there! But their headlines don't always define the way I grew up living there. It was and still is incredibly multicultural, with many tenth-generation Chinese and Greek families living in Darwin. Because it is so close to South-East Asia we have many Filipino, Malaysian, Indonesian and Timorese families in Darwin and this is represented through the diverse mouth-watering cuisines at the local markets.

So, while there is definitely that side of home, I am a proud Larrakia and Tiwi woman born and bred on the land that is now called Darwin. Darwin and its surrounding areas continue to be the ancestral lands of my great-grandmother, Dedja Batcho. Nana Dedja was the daughter of a Larrakia woman and a Malay fisherman. Dedja was taken by force from her family to the Kahlin Compound, a mission for 'half-caste' children. Similar to 'Indian Removal' policies throughout North America, Australian Aboriginal children were routinely removed from their families and put into institutions to be assimilated into the coloniser's culture.

Nana Dedja was one of the many Aboriginal women who were trained at one of these institutions to be domestic servants for White people. After 'training', Dedja went out into the workforce. One of her relationships was with my great-grandfather, a Tiwi artist called Stanislaus Puruntatameri; they had three children—Lucy, Yula and Keith—and then separated and both remarried. She had fallen in and out of love many times, but had managed to keep her children together. My maternal grandmother, Lucy, grew up with her siblings—Victor Williams, Bertie Batcho, Lindy Quall, Keith Batcho, Yula Williams, Mary Raymond and Rona Alley. I hope I don't upset family members for not mentioning other names on my family tree but, the problem is, I'm related to half the Northern Territory. I used to wonder why Nana Lucy and my mother used to be so pedantic about the cleanliness of the house. It's because in my mother's time they lived in Aboriginal housing and their homes were constantly inspected by authorities. It was also one of the main reasons children were wrenched out of homes. The cleanliness of your house was what kept authorities away from your family.

It didn't matter what mix you were—if you were an Aboriginal child born of an interracial relationship, like my great-grandmother Dedja, you were considered less Aboriginal, which meant you were a step closer to whiteness. While these Government policies were amended in each State and Territory, the overall agenda was to breed out whatever 'Aboriginality' was left. We have a handful of crazy settlers who attempt to deny in the media that this ever happened, despite the fact many men and women who experienced this trauma in their childhood are still alive today. Many conservative journalists and politicians still hold the belief that it was for the Aboriginal children's benefit, but it's only been since 2007 that the Australian Government has acknowledged that the displacement has left many Aboriginal families longing for family and country. It's sad to say that every Aboriginal person has been affected by this to some degree. Intergenerational trauma is a very real thing and the impact ripples on. It's even sadder that while the policy has since been removed, Aboriginal children are still being taken from families, and caring relatives are being overlooked by the foster-care system.

I get my Larrakia and Tiwi blood from my mother. My mum was, and still is, a staunch Aboriginal woman who loves her family fiercely. I get my predominantly Irish Roman Catholic heritage from my father. Dad is extremely affectionate and has a very good sense of humour, even if his jokes can be stereotypically Dad-like. I'm incredibly close to my parents. At home I've never had to choose between my mother's Aboriginality or my father's European ancestry. I have never had anything but love and care from both sides of my family. My biracial background doesn't dilute my lived experience or diminish my connection to my land.

Growing up around my mother's family and community meant being Aboriginal was never something to be ashamed of. Both my parents completely normalised this for me. They say it takes a village to raise a child, and that was certainly my experience. My grandparents, uncles and Aunties always stepped in to babysit when my parents needed them to. My cousins were often at my house. My mother would take me out to land-claim meetings, the Larrakia having one of the longest ongoing land claims in Australia. Larrakia country covers most of the Darwin region. Many of the pictures of me as a baby were taken on a tarpaulin or a swag out bush when my family were camping or fishing.

For me, my family, my country and my history are what define me. And the safety my parents gave me in my childhood to express myself fearlessly and to understand where I'd come from is what I believe helped fuel my desire to perform.

Even though I moved south to pursue a career in acting, the Territory has never left me. It's home. The place I go to when I want to feel whole again. The people, the pace, the food, the colours, the tranquillity—they are everything I need to replenish myself so I can step back up to take on life's challenges. When I go home to Darwin it forces me to reflect on who I am and what I want. As thrilling as my life is in the 'big smoke' of Melbourne, I can sometimes lose my way. The noise and bustle can overwhelm, and it can be particularly discombobulating when I'm travelling constantly between Melbourne and Sydney, where the bulk of the major film and television productions tend to be made.

For me, remembering who I am and where I have come from is very important and it helps me stay true to myself. Though my name may sound like a character out of a Charles Dickens novel, I'm a Larrakia Tiwi woman. I don't claim to be from an African diaspora, but like Torres Strait Islanders, Fijians, Papuans, New Caledonians and Solomon Islanders and many other Indigenous groups across Melanesia, I identify as coming from a Black diaspora.

As a kid I had picture books of Dreaming stories. I was given an African-American Cabbage Patch doll—called Sasha— who was the same colour as my mum. I nursed, cuddled and held her on my hip the same way my Nana and Aunties held babies in the family. All of this helped me understand myself. Understand that I was complicated and that there is beauty in that complexity. Stories helped me separate valuable life wisdom from something thoughtless that came out of someone's mouth.

I learned way back at a primary school disco—when my obsession with the Spice Girls forced me to recognise that people impose expectations because of skin colour (no, I don't want to wear the leopard print and stick my tongue out and be Scary Spice, I want a pink flowery dress and glitter hairspray, just like Baby)—that I was not going to conform to other people's limitations or expectations.

I grew up with hardworking, self-assured parents. My dad worked in local Government and my mum worked at ATSIC, a Government department related to Aboriginal affairs, before becoming an Aboriginal Education Officer at both my primary and secondary schools. While my parents might not have chosen a creative path, they always appreciated art and it was because of them that I enjoyed stories.

When I was young my dad read to me before bed, often with funny voices so that he would know I was paying attention to the words. My favourite was his attempt at a French accent, which I found delightfully terrible. He didn't need the voices, because I would be quick to correct him when he went off script because, even though I couldn't yet read, I knew my favourite books by heart. He would pretend to fall asleep, snoring loudly until I squealed with glee, 'Wake up, Dad!' and he would wake up in mock-surprise. This was well before Jeff from The Wiggles pretended to have narcolepsy. I'm sure Jeff stole the idea from my dad. Dad would chuckle when I told him off for sleeping on the job. Bless him, acting is not one of his strengths. Quite often my unimpressed mum would burst into the room and remind Dad that his already lively and opinionated daughter didn't need to be more riled up before bed.

I lived in a traditional household, and it was expected of my parents by their families that while both my parents worked, the main childrearing would be done by Mum. That was just the time it was. This doesn't mean I didn't have a great relationship with my dad (and still have). But because he worked so much, reading before bed was our time together.

I think I'm a little bit like my dad when it comes to work. I'm really in my element when I am busy. When I'm working I know exactly what I need to do. Anything outside of that, I need prompting and help.

When I wanted to know who I was and better understand the people around me, I turned to books, movies and television. I've always struggled to brush off what others thought of me. I just cared too much. I remember when I was twelve and I realised I didn't have the same growth spurt as the other girls. As Alicia and most of the other girls in my class began to stretch out, I knew it wasn't going to happen for me. Thankfully there were a few other kids who were in the same position as me, but it was still something I was deeply insecure about. One of the more popular girls in the class had said to me, 'You know, if you were just a little taller, guys would really go for you.' For the record, there was no malice in the way she said this. But rather than taking the comment with a grain of salt, I believed it to be true—that I would be taken more seriously or seen as beautiful if I were taller. Boys in my class had picked this up as a sore point, so they would tease me about it.

I went to school with most of the same people from year one to year nine. Before I go on I should add, most of the boys in my class were super mischievous. To paint a picture of what utter shitheads they could be, I will share a story of the time we learned the Indonesian word for 'flower' in year seven. To be fair, we really should have been learning Kunwinjku instead, since we were all on the land of the Mirarr, but that's the Australian education system babyyyyyyyy! Even if he wasn't in a position to teach us Kunwinjku, our pengajar should have been across the fact that the word for 'flower' in Bahasa is 'bunga', which just so happens to also be the Kunwinjku word for 'penis'. Once he had written 'bunga' up on the board and told the class to 'repeat after me', the boys erupted into laughter, shouting to each other, 'Hey look, that's you on the board there!' 'Shut up, that's you, dickhead!' Our pengajar turned bright red and roared, 'What is so funny?' which only made them laugh harder. Look, I have to admit that story is quite funny, but I can imagine teaching our class must have been a nightmare.

Mum and Dad both come from huge families, so they were better at letting things like my concern about my height slide. What didn't help was that relatives would always make me go back-to-back with my cousins and then say, 'Miranda, you haven't grown at all!' And I hadn't. Despite this, neither of my parents could understand why I would build up such a complex over it.

Dad was one of twelve, Mum the eldest of eight. With such a big extended family, you'd think I'd have a thicker skin. My cousins were so used to taunting one another, naturally I was always the next target. I was an only child so, even though I was told not to react, I didn't always handle it well and, like my dad, I have an awful poker face, so everyone knew exactly how I felt. I had to learn how to deal with those taunts, share my toys and my parents' attention. They weren't easy lessons.

Still, I'm grateful to have so many cousins. I remember at age five asking my mum when I was going to get a little brother or sister, and her sitting me on her lap and saying, 'I'm really sorry, but Mummy can't give you that.'

I later found out it had been a long road for her to fall pregnant with me. There were many complications during labour, and she had almost died. My friend Benjamin Law (who wrote the wonderful book *The Family Law* that is now a television series) calls up his mother every birthday to thank her for all the pain she went through to give birth to him. I really need to take up this tradition. My mother is an incredibly generous mother and Aunty. It's clear that her sometimes stern ways come from a place of love. That said, I was envious of the way my friends and cousins could distract their parents from their own disobedience by saying, 'But what about [insert sibling's name here]? They did [insert offence here]!' I had no one to deflect to. I could never get away with skipping school or not handing in homework, because my mother would be on my back straightaway. No mercy.

But because of the home I grew up in, one that gave me the safety to be myself, I was also empowered to stand up for myself. My parents kept a diary of all the funny things I said to them as a kid. My dad told me that one day when I was four years old I walked into the dining room and he said to me, 'Good morning, my golden girl,' and I told him straight out, 'I'm not a golden girl, I'm a Black girl.' So, that was that.

Poor bloke never got a break. Here's an extract from his journal from another day:

16.11.1992

At breakfast, Miranda wanted to know the name of the box she was sitting on (she sits on a box to give her height at the table so she can eat easily). I said, 'That's Tupperware, my sugar plum,' to which she replied in an abrasive tone, 'Not Sugar Plum! Am I a fruit?' I said no, she wasn't a fruit, so that settled that; but I couldn't stop laughing at myself. She rebutted a sexist remark very well, even if I meant it as a form of affection.

Not a sugar plum. Not a golden girl. A Black woman from day dot.

Not only does it feel completely normal for me to say I'm Aboriginal, it is something I like about myself and is something that can never be separated from who I fundamentally am.

CHAPTER TWO

NO PLAN B

WHEN I WAS FIVE, MY DAD GOT A JOB AS TOWN CLERK at Jabiru Town Council (it's now West Arnhem Regional Council), which crushed my dreams of becoming a ballerina. When we moved from Darwin, I discovered Jabiru didn't care for ballet. I, in turn, didn't care for the ancient rock formations, the breathtaking waterfalls or the majestic wildlife that lived across the ever-expanding floodplains. I wanted the pink tutu, pointy shoes and nothing else. My mum had tried to make the move more appealing by mentioning the tap-dance group that got together after school. I was so offended that my mother would even attempt to sign me up, I walked off in a huff, disgusted at the thought that this backwater had tap-dance classes but not ballet. My dreams of becoming a ballerina had been destroyed.

Maybe to distract me from my tutu obsession, my parents began a Friday-night tradition of riding our bikes up to the local video shop and picking a movie to watch together. (I'll take this moment to humbly brag that I have now surpassed their knowledge of Hollywood actors and the films they've been in. Some now call me MTDb.) I absorbed their interest in art—paintings, songs, books, films, television shows and plays—which naturally morphed into my putting shows on in the lounge room. I remember choreographing and dancing to the song 'Friend Like Me' from Disney's *Aladdin* for my grandfather's birthday. My parents, cousins and Nana were all sitting watching, and I remember the little thrill as I brought out my stereo and pressed play. I was really proud to perform for him after I had spent all afternoon on the routine. I had never understood this feeling until then—that buzz you get when you're about to perform. I hadn't dressed up, because it was all about having an audience. I know, *such* an only child.

The love of performing was only heightened when I'd visit my cousins in Sydney. Aunty Linda still has tapes of me and her sons, my cousins Guy and Nicholas, using their video recorder to film not only the important news of the week, but the people we thought were going to save us from evil. When I was a reporter, I played a scorpion expert. Because that's what everyone wants to know about every week: what scorpions are up to. Power Rangers were big at the time, and Guy and Nick were both dressed as them. I can't remember how they had managed to break into my character's house, but once they had, I kicked both their arses.

At my Aunty Jenny and Uncle Bob's house, there was an amazing dress-ups box. It was my cousin Olivia, who was my age, who made me want to do ballet because she was going to classes. I loved wearing her pink tutu. Olivia and my cousin Louise and I would make up dance routines to our favourite songs.

I was thirteen when the actor Aaron Pedersen came to my school in Jabiru. Aaron was one of the stars of the Australian TV show *Water Rats*, which was huge in the nineties. It was a show about police solving crimes on the water. It was years ahead of its time. Aaron was in Jabiru to conduct a drama workshop with us kids. Here was someone telling me I could change who I was through acting. Who showed me how to walk and talk differently. To become someone else. I loved it.

At some moment in that workshop I realised … this was Aaron's job. It's not that I wasn't aware of home-grown films and television. I absolutely adored *Strictly Ballroom*, *Muriel's Wedding* and *Priscilla, Queen of the Desert*. But meeting Aaron Pedersen made the idea of becoming a performer in Australia possible for me. Like I said earlier, you don't aspire to be what you cannot see. Aaron made me see. I could actually be paid for all of the things I enjoyed doing at home—dressing up and putting on funny voices. Except rather than do it badly in my lounge room, it could become a craft. I couldn't change being short or being Aboriginal, and I didn't want to, but through taking on the role of someone else, maybe I wouldn't have to.

While I grew up being proud of everything I am, one of the big reasons I embraced acting was that I knew that being Aboriginal seemed to bother a lot of non-Indigenous people around me. Performing reminded me that I didn't have to deny any aspect of myself. I had found an outlet, not only a way to articulate who I was but how to care for myself when I did so. In saying this, finding my voice didn't happen overnight. It's definitely a process, one that I want to evolve and grow over time.

My adolescence had been a real test of courage. I remember being fourteen and being asked by a boy in my class, 'So, Miranda, why do you say you're Aboriginal?' This was a strange question to me, because it was completely normal to call myself that. It was what my family wanted me to call myself. But there was only one other boy in the class who had a non-Indigenous dad like me. The rest of the Black kids in my year had two Aboriginal parents. So, I was a point of interest. I struggled to find the language to deconstruct the way I had grown up, the way I saw the world around me. I shrugged and said, 'Because I am.' But this guy needed an answer. 'But your dad's White,' the boy pointed out. 'Why don't you say that you're part-Aboriginal?' Honestly, we were doing pottery. I couldn't understand why he would want to have a conversation about the affect of colonisation over moulding clay. I simply told him it was derogatory, but he still didn't understand—why was it derogatory to embrace my father's heritage as much as my mother's, since I love them both equally? I was not, and still am not, a damn cake mix. I am not a percentage.

This inquisition really got to me. I told my parents when I got home, and it happened to coincide with a speech I had to prepare for English, with the very unfortunate and not-well-thought-out name of 'Oral Assessment'. Teachers … I know how hard you work, but please don't call an assignment for fourteen-year-olds an 'Oral Assessment'.

When it came to preparing my speech for English class, I wasn't really equipped to illustrate how the true history of this land informs the lives of Aboriginal and Torres Strait Islanders.

Thankfully, my parents filled in a lot of gaps. In fact, when I wanted to understand why our Prime Minister at the time, John Howard, wanted to claim Terra Nullius, it was Mum who said, 'He's trying to tell us that Aboriginal people were never here before the English.' It was the most political I had ever seen my mum. As grateful as I was that my parents had kept an open dialogue through books and general conversation, it was something I was also hoping to learn at school. Sure, I was taught pockets of history, but the remainder of the time I was learning about Ancient Egypt and Medieval England. As fascinating as both these histories are, I was burning to know about our own. When we got to choose what we wanted to write about in our Social Studies class, I decided to research Eddie Mabo and the *Native Title Act*. Since I wasn't going to learn about it from the teacher, I decided to find out for myself. I remember my year-five teacher a few years earlier teaching us about Australia's neighbours, where we touched on the cultures that came from Indonesia, Papua New Guinea and New Zealand. I know there's a lot more but we covered a lot from those three countries, and it was because of this that at that time I decided to do a Social Studies project on the Maori of New Zealand. Because, again, it was another ancient culture that we weren't going to learn about and I knew that while their culture was inherently different, their experience with colonisation was similar to ours. I remember my friend pointing out that I always picked out 'Indigenous things' but I wanted something to take out into adult life. I mean, wasn't that what school was supposed to prepare me for?

I know I'm not alone in this experience; a lot of people in my generation have left school without knowing about the history of this country that existed before Captain Cook arrived. But having my ancestors' lives completely erased from the history I was taught made me more vulnerable when I was asked to give up my blackness and just be Australian. The whole way Australia is set up is still designed for me to do that. But even if I did deny being Aboriginal, or say that I was 'half', my family would still be in exactly the same place. The gap in health and education would still exist. Some non-Indigenous people would ask me where my dark relatives came from.

Thank God my English teacher Ms Vandermark was deeply committed to educating us all on the history of Kakadu. I remember learning in her class about the Macassans, who traded trepang (sea slug) with the Yolngu across Eastern Arnhem Land, but also of Truganini in Tasmania and other Aboriginal rebels. Ms Vandermark did an incredible job given how isolated we were and how broken the education system is.

Knowing how unruly the boys were, knowing that the education system had left kids like me behind, I wanted to get up in front of the class in English and say what I never got to say to the boy in art class. I remember my dad staying up with me until 1am to help me break down why being part-, half-, quarter- or any-other-fraction-Aboriginal was wrong to say to any kid like me.

By the time I got up in front of the class, I was fired up. I had something to say and I was going to say it. I challenged the class on why I was expected to choose between my parents' identities but the White kids who had two White parents were saved from this labour. I asked why they didn't have to decipher what kind of White they were. Of course, the boys didn't want to be told this and by the end of my presentation I was booed and taunted. I thought that I would only have to cop it that day and they would sleep it off, but the bullying got worse. Over the next days and weeks my chair was pulled from under me, my hair was tugged and I was called awful names like 'gin-bag' and 'nigger'.

Just sitting there and taking it would have made me hate myself even more. I didn't want to go to school anymore. I stood up for myself as best I could but the constant arguing finally got to the point where the year coordinator called me and some of the boys into a meeting to sort it out. At the end of it we still disagreed with one another, but this was the teacher's way of telling all of us to rein it in. The boys stopped hassling me because they didn't want to deal with another meeting.

I'm telling this story because in my early teens I really struggled to articulate who I was, and whenever I tried to explain I would end up feeling like I had alienated myself from the people around me. My parents and friends just wanted me to turn the other cheek. So, when we moved out of Jabiru and back to Darwin, I decided to try out their advice. I made friendships with many considerate people at Darwin High School. There were lots of compassionate and intelligent students at the school. But the suburbs surrounding that school didn't have a lot of Aboriginal and Torres Strait Islander families living in them, so there weren't many Black students attending that school. I was one of the few. My grandmother had moved into the area before it had become gentrified, and we were now living in that house. At school, I was made to feel like my Aboriginality was a burden on everyone else, so, like a lot of sixteen year olds, I acknowledged everything else but my cultural connection to my traditional lands, just to fit in. This was despite the fact that my grandmother had been born under a tree where the high school now stands.

The everyday racism that me and my family experienced in the Northern Territory doesn't look like angry people carrying torches, pitchforks and white blankets. Whenever I spoke from an honest place about the way I saw things, I was more often than not met with a lot of hostility or denial. It was at high school where I realised that I would be regularly considering the feelings of a non-Indigenous person if they were made to acknowledge race.

Also, despite my mother being a remarkably strong woman, she was quite selective when she chose to be outspoken. Even though she was very understanding, she was of the belief that keeping my head down and focusing on my school work was the best way to deal with some of the micro-aggressions I faced at school. It was how a lot of the women in my mother's family survived. While self-care is so important, I didn't always agree with just letting things slide—where could I place my frustration and resentment when I felt othered? I needed an outlet when I was misunderstood.

There is a spark in me that has always been determined that I will be more than the limitations people placed on me for being a short, Aboriginal girl. I didn't think being short, being Aboriginal or being a girl was ever an issue for me, but when people were reminded that I was all three, it would become an issue for them. It was bigger than me, too. I was often made to choose between my dad's identity and my mother's, my mother's being a larger threat.

Listening to Aaron Pedersen, an Arrernte–Arabana man, ignited that spark. Acting sounded like the best job in the world and I couldn't picture myself doing anything else. I guess that's pretty decisive for a thirteen year old, but I've always loathed having to do things I don't want to do. If I ever protested about completing chores or homework on a hated subject, my parents would bleakly point out that most of adult life consisted of having to do things you didn't want to do. If that were the case, I thought, then I would resent being a grown-up a whole lot less if I chose a career where I was excited to wake up and go to work.

I can't remember when exactly I told my mum that I wanted to be an actor, but my parents never stopped me from chasing that as a career. Mum started collecting issues of *Deadly Vibe* magazine for me. Often handed out in schools, this magazine was a part of Vibe Australia, a Black-run media outlet. It went out to the wider Aboriginal and Torres Strait Islander community, namely school kids. There were articles about eating a healthy, balanced diet and the importance of going to school every day. It was about empowering kids and sharing stories about Indigenous creatives. It is where

I learned about Deborah Mailman and Leah Purcell. Seeing experienced, professional actors making a name for themselves in the mainstream media planted the idea that my home and my community would still be there if I left; it made it a less scary thing to contemplate. I knew I could always come back to country.

To be a really great actor you have to be given the permission to do it by others. My parents were a big reason for my bravery. I'm grateful that incessantly asking to be granted this freedom of expression has paid off. It doesn't always for performers in the industry, so it is important to me that whenever I'm given an opportunity, I take it with both hands and run with it.

Before we had moved back to Darwin, my mum happened to come across a pamphlet for the National Institute of Dramatic Art (NIDA), the prestigious Australian institution that boasts alumni such as Cate Blanchett and Hugo Weaving. They toured their short courses nation-wide to all the capital cities in Australia, and Mum signed me up for one in Darwin during my school holidays. The teacher was Wendy Strehlow, a kind woman who had also graduated from NIDA and gone on to a successful acting career. Every day for the week, we would start by doing a salute to the sun. It was the first time I ever did yoga. During these workshops I realised that while acting was still a lot of fun and you could use your imagination, it was no longer a hobby for the people who made a life out of it. I saw that there is a discipline behind an actor's instincts.

My mum could see that I was in to this acting caper in a big way, so she signed me up for more classes in Sydney—after we had Christmas with my dad's side of the family in Engadine in the Shire. Dad had to go back to work in the Northern Territory in the new year but Mum and I stayed with my Aunty, who, like my mum, was also called Barbara, so I could attend NIDA's summer school. This was when I got a real taste of what life would be like as a performer. Not just because of what we were learning in class, but the fact that preparing for a performance becomes all-consuming. I would be woken up by my mother at 6am and we would be on a train, then a bus for the roughly two-and-a-half-hour trip to NIDA. By the time I'd get back to my Aunty Barb's again, I was told to shower, eat, then go to bed. My mum would not let me stay up to watch TV, even if it was school holidays. So, I'm a drama nerd because of her.

Later that year, I had my first ever audition for a film. Open casting calls were being held for the role of Molly in *Rabbit-Proof Fence*. Phillip Noyce, the director of *Clear and Present Danger*, *Dead Calm* and *The Bone Collector*, was making a film adaptation of Doris Pilkington Garimara's book. The production was doing an Australia-wide search, and had come to Darwin to hold auditions. The story followed the escape of Doris's mother, Molly, from Moore River Native Settlement. Just like my great-grandmother Dedja, Molly was taken from her mother's arms to be assimilated into Western society, so the story resonated with me and I wanted the part of Molly so much.

It wasn't much of an audition per se, it was basically an interview in front of a camera. I was so nervous. I talked about where I came from and who my family were. When I was asked if I spoke any of my ancestors' language, I was honest and told them no. It saddened me that I couldn't express myself in this way and that it was something that had been out of my control. The last speaker of the Larrakia language had passed away in the early 1970s and took the language with his spirit. Obviously there are traditional words we know, especially when we talk about plants and animals, but this isn't something that can be spoken fluently. As much as I wanted the role, something told me that I wasn't right for the part. Then I received a letter in the mail saying that unfortunately I was not chosen for the part of Molly. Even though I knew I wasn't right for it, I was devastated, but my mother wouldn't let me feel sorry for myself. She reminded me that this would happen a lot if I really wanted to become a professional actor, and I couldn't give up at the first rejection. The film came out the following year. A 'Making Of' documentary was on TV in the lead-up to the release of the movie, and watching it I saw that Everlyn Sampi was just so right as Molly. She was a natural. Not only did the camera love her, this Bardi woman was clearly cast because of the inner strength she carried. That's when I came to the realisation that a rejection didn't mean I couldn't be a good actor, but the essence I could bring to a role might not always be the right fit. I could continue to evolve as a performer, but the way we are cast can be completely subjective. So, I didn't get the role but I fell more in love with the idea of acting.

I was fifteen when we moved back to Darwin from Jabiru. The high school in Jabiru only went up to year ten. Most of the miners who lived in the town sent their kids off to boarding school for the last two years of their education, but my mum was keen to be back with family on country. By this point I really, really wanted to move down to Sydney and attend a performing-arts school such as The McDonald College or Newtown High School of the Performing Arts. I practically begged my mother to allow me to be a child star, but she refused. I was going to have a normal childhood and graduate from a normal high school whether I wanted to or not.

It wasn't a bad decision. Darwin High School has an extensive Dance and Drama faculty and I signed up for all of it. The entire population of Jabiru had been about 1100 people, give or take, and this was about the number of students at Darwin High. It felt exciting and vibrant and I was ready to push myself. This was the sea change I had been hoping for. I was diving right in with acting as my focus, so after each school day finished I would go to Corrugated Iron Youth Arts, an incredible local youth theatre company.

Jeremy Rice was my main tutor at Corrugated Iron and he was the one who told me that to be a good actor you need to absorb everything—watch films and plays, read everything. Jeremy made it clear that it was more than just chilling on the couch, and that I should be actively interpreting the way in which a story was structured. At this point I had no idea how to write plays or screenplays. But understanding what stories stayed with me and why was a good starting point. It was the best advice and I found it easy to embrace.

Because Jeremy was a NIDA alumni he recognised my passion for the craft and knew that an audition piece was important, so he taught me Juliet's soliloquy from *Romeo and Juliet*. It was the biggest challenge I'd ever had as a performer up until then, but having the soliloquy in my back pocket became a big asset for future auditions. Also, I was obsessed with Claire Danes and that angel costume in Baz Luhrmann's film, so Jeremy also gave me the belief that I could play this role. My Drama teacher at Darwin High School, Sally Crawford, told me about the Bell Shakespeare company, a premier theatre company based in Sydney. Established by actor/director John Bell, the company brought Shakespeare plays and other classics to regional areas, including Darwin. Because I fly so much for work now, I can easily forget how big the country is. When I Google nerdy facts such as 'How many European countries fit into Australia', I'm reminded just how ridiculously big it is. The sheer size of the continent makes it incredibly difficult for those living outside Sydney and Melbourne to be exposed to theatre of Bell Shakespeare's calibre. It is incredibly ambitious of Bell Shakespeare to tour actors to these isolated parts of the country, but it is what the company is renowned for.

Sally encouraged me to audition for the Australia Post Bell Shakespeare Regional Scholarship. There would be only two recipients out of the whole country, and whoever was accepted got to travel down to Sydney and watch the rehearsal process of the company's latest production. I arrived at Darwin Entertainment Centre, heart pounding, nerves taut. I don't remember the woman's name who ran the auditions but she was incredibly encouraging. Even though I had been to Sydney many times to visit my family and take part in workshops, the opportunity to see actors doing this as a profession and not a hobby was something that would change my life. A month later, I was short-listed. My mum reminded me to stay philosophical, and that to be short-listed was in itself a wonderful achievement. Another month passed before I received another letter in the mail. I was at recess with my friends when I opened it. It was a letter from Bell Shakespeare congratulating me on being one of the two recipients of the scholarship. This was huge. I felt like I was floating on air. It was sheer disbelief: this went across the entire country, and they chose me.

I flew down to Sydney and met Ben Cooper, the other recipient who was from Bathurst in the Central Tablelands of western New South Wales. The company's latest production was Carlo Goldoni's *The Servant of Two Masters*. Adapted by Australian playwright Nick Enright, this eighteenth-century *commedia dell'arte* play was highly physical with lots of slapstick comedy. I had never seen acting like it. Watching the performers rehearse was electric. It was like observing athletes at the Olympics—they were at the top of their game. The actors had the freedom to do a lot of improvising around the script and they would come out and fearlessly make a hilarious character choice that would leave the director, John Bell himself, in stitches. It was magical to watch all these actors think so quickly on their feet. Each and every one of them was mesmerising. A few of the cast members would step out of rehearsals to conduct workshops with Ben and me. Ben was very playful and cheeky, which made the workshops less intimidating because he wasn't scared to put himself out there. I had a harder time hiding my insecurities because of how new it all was. I was invited to take up space, something that had never really happened to me before. I didn't know how they did it but I wanted nothing more than to have that kind of craft: that state of being incredibly present and reacting honestly with what was unfolding in front of you. Even though I still had a lot to learn, the week I had in those rehearsals made my dreams feel all the more tangible.

At the end of that year I graduated from Darwin High School. I had always struggled academically, particularly with maths, and I had over-committed to extra-curricular things as most Drama nerds do—but I managed to pass year twelve. I had nowhere near the marks that would get me into a Medicine or Law degree, but it would be enough to be accepted into the National Institute of Dramatic Art, which was the only thing I truly wanted.

Thankfully, this prestigious acting school held auditions in every capital city in Australia. The auditions in Darwin were in November, only weeks after I graduated. Kevin Jackson, the then acting tutor of NIDA, was in charge of these auditions held in Darwin. While he was very impressed with the pieces I performed—I put my heart and soul into Juliet's soliloquy 'Gallop Apace'—I didn't get an offer that year. I was only seventeen and I had just come out of one institution and wanted to go into another. I was shattered, but I was told that if I was going to reflect life in my acting, I had to go out and live it first. I had applied to do other tertiary courses but I was completely unmotivated to go back into a classroom for anything other than Drama. Even though I hadn't been accepted, Kevin enrolled me into the NIDA short courses that were held in Sydney over the summer. Mum paid for the flights and accommodation, and Kevin was kind enough to waive the fee for the course. I was touched that he could see the passion and drive I had for story and craft. And I felt that was an encouragement to keep trying.

Once I had a taste of what the three-year NIDA course would be like, I knew I wouldn't put my heart into any other tertiary course. I needed to work and earn some money. Because I had no prior experience in retail or hospitality, I ended up working at McDonald's. It was the last place I wanted to be, but it turned out to be the very place I needed to be. Everyone I worked with was down-to-earth and kind. They were all different ages and backgrounds, and having them around made work seem less arduous. I guess it was because we were all smelling the same deep-fryer oil. I had turned eighteen my first year out of high school, and I felt empowered to be earning my own money. I was buying things I wanted, going out to clubs and performing in local plays in Darwin. I truly felt like my own woman.

November came around again, and Jeremy offered to help with my audition. Of course I was going to try to get into NIDA again. Another person auditioning that year was a young Aboriginal man named Travis. He had performed in a local production and had made all the young women around me swoon when they saw it. He was Darwin's heartthrob. He also started going out with a girl who had gone to Darwin High with me, Daphne. Travis and I both rehearsed our scenes with Jeremy, and we helped each other with lines. As usual, the day of the auditions I was very nervous. Kevin had returned to Darwin and seemed pleased that I was there to give it another try. But there was no guarantee I would be accepted, and I had made no plan B if I wasn't. I hadn't auditioned for other drama schools, which didn't have the same amount of funding as NIDA to travel to places like Darwin. I didn't know anyone in Perth, Adelaide, Melbourne or Brisbane but I knew Sydney and NIDA fairly well. NIDA was it for me at that moment. I remember walking with Travis down the main street in Darwin after we had auditioned. We didn't say anything. We were both unsure of how we had done and all we could do was wait.

A few weeks passed, and it was the night of my mum's Christmas party. She and a few of the other teachers and admin staff from Darwin High were going on a cruise around the harbour. Much to my parents' annoyance, I had been partying too much to go and get my licence, so when I had to be somewhere I would catch public transport or my parents would give me a lift or pick me up. Because my mother had told me she was going out and couldn't pick me up, I was totally confused when one of my co-workers, Hao, said to me, 'Miranda, your mum is here,' just as I clocked off.

I had a Happy Meal to go when I got in the car. Mum didn't even let me get out the question 'What are you doing here?' before she shushed me and told me to listen. She held up Dad's old tape recorder and pressed play. It was the head of acting at NIDA. She had recorded the voice message he'd left on our answering machine. Yes, answering machine. I am aware of my age and how old school it is to use landline phones and answering machines. If my younger cousins are reading this, stop laughing! He congratulated me to say that I had successfully been accepted into first year at NIDA. Was this a prank? It would have been the cruellest thing Mum could have ever done to me. I think I accused her multiple times of making it up, and she denied it every time. Finally it hit me, I screamed and threw my Happy Meal up in the air. A couple had walked past and the woman frowned in confusion, but I didn't care. Then my mum began to cry. She said, 'I'm so happy for you.' We held on to each other for a very long time. I still couldn't believe it. I was going to be a student at the most esteemed drama school in the country! And it was all because my parents helped me with my dream.

CHAPTER THREE

INTO THE FIRE

I WON'T LIE—MY TIME AT NIDA WAS A REAL BAPTISM OF fire. I'd like to tell you I came into my own over those three years, but that didn't happen until well after I graduated. But what I learned about myself, the industry and my craft was well worth it, even though I struggled many times.

I was so happy to be offered a place but nervous about what was to come. I wanted to be good at it all. I was thrilled to find out that Travis had been accepted as well. It turned out, we were the only Aboriginal people in the year, so I was grateful to have a brother go on this journey with me. I remember someone introducing Travis and me as 'the

Aboriginal students' to the rest of the class, telling the others that we would be offered more roles in the industry than anyone else who graduated with us. Regardless of whether they meant any offence, it came across to me as if Travis and I would have a smoother run because we wouldn't have to rely on talent or ability. Black roles would be written for us. I was confused because I thought we had both been accepted because of our talent and ability to learn. Not because we were Aboriginal.

While it would turn out that I would be successful in my career after graduating, I baulked at that intro. It didn't feel right being pitted against people, like *The Hunger Games*. Also, being singled out in this way made me feel as if Travis and I had been given two spots in the year out of charity. The people in my year had no idea of the fire I carried in me. But I won't spend too long speculating on what the others thought of me, because I'm sure they don't look back and wonder what I thought of them. That introduction, however, got under my skin and made me feel like I wasn't meant to be there. And I didn't know what to do about that, there was no one I felt I could share my thoughts with. Travis was most definitely in my corner, but I didn't want to bother anyone with my problems. Everyone was just trying to get through.

Not having family or friends close by to ground me, I retreated further into my shell. My voice teacher mistook my silence in the class as attitude, and failed me in the first term. I made matters worse when I was late for one of our end-of-term presentations because I had forgotten we had to wear all black that day. When I realised, I raced back home to change—making me very late. Despite the fact that aside from this particular day I always managed to turn up on time, lateness was never accepted, and my voice teacher was furious. The first report they gave me on my work told me I sounded like 'nails being dragged across a chalkboard' and I needed to get rid of my 'Territory accent'. I felt like, if I was to pass, I had to give up everything that made me confident. My hometown. My community. My identity. It left me confused and unsure.

Confidence is everything for an actor. So, as you can imagine, because my confidence was now lacking, I was terrible. It didn't help when I got up to sing in music class and the tutor asked my classmates, 'So, what did Miranda do wrong here?' I got the sense I was being taught from a place of fear rather than one of encouragement. I started to question whether I was getting worse. What's so wrong with encouragement anyway? It doesn't have to be about empty validation, it's about articulating to someone whether or not they are on the right track—in a positive way.

My days at NIDA have made me very skilled at deciphering criticism that isn't constructive—but back then I really struggled to hide my insecurities. It all came out in my voice. I spoke with head resonance rather than with grounded technique from my belly because I wanted to make myself smaller than I already was. I failed Voice as a subject every term that first year. I noticed that a lot of the students who passed with flying colours were from Adelaide, who said *dance, chance* and *France* like they'd just come from an English high tea.

There were many people in my year who looked to England to understand themselves, so they found it easier to relate to the characters we all played on stage. I was used to Caucasian characters being considered the epitome of the universal human experience in art; but after three years of reading nothing but works from Western literature, I began to see less and less of myself in the stories to which we were applying our craft. Most of my classmates had attained other degrees, had travelled the world and had fallen in and out of love—things I had never done. Everyone came across as much more self-assured than I ever did or felt.

I was baffled by how disconnected my fellow students were about our own history. Sure the school system let them down, but I also got the strong impression no one wanted to know. The most non-European we got in first year was when a group of us performed a short play called *Amandla*, about apartheid in South Africa. I remember one actor in the class saying something along the lines of, 'It makes you appreciate that there hasn't been the same kind of warfare here.' I didn't have the confidence to share with her our own version of apartheid in Australia. When a teacher made a point about how uneducated most Australians are on their colonial history, he quizzed us with questions such as what year the HMS *Endeavour* arrived (1770) and who the ship's botanist was (Joseph Banks). As I, the Aboriginal girl, answered all the questions about 'the colony', I realised that the people surrounding me didn't have to think about our shared history as much as I did because they don't have to live with it.

There was one thing that came full circle for me. Phillip Noyce, the director of *Rabbit-Proof Fence*, came to speak to the students at NIDA. Afterwards, Kevin Jackson, our acting teacher, introduced me and I managed to blubber through my star-struck state to ask him if he had any advice for an Aboriginal woman entering the industry like I hoped to. And he smiled and said to me, 'Start to tell your own stories.' I had no idea how to do that, but that fire inside me lit up again.

I was on probation in second year because I had returned from Christmas up in Darwin with the same accent I had arrived with the year before. A lot of my educators believed I had taken a step backwards. My stagecraft was not particularly great either. Let me give you an example of how terrible I was. I had been cast as both Charmian and Octavia in William Shakespeare's *Antony and Cleopatra*. This meant I had to change from an Egyptian to a Roman as fast as lightning. As if that wasn't confusing enough, there was a set of stairs that moved, and we were performing on a raised stage. There was a blackout for the scene change and I stepped out onto … air. People watching just saw me disappear like Wile E Coyote into a canyon. My legs, butt and ego were all bruised from the fall and I was in so much pain that all I could do was crawl. While I had been given comfort and an ice pack, the show, of course, had to go on. I didn't have time to change because I spent the time applying Voltaren to my arse-cheek so I went back on in the same Egyptian costume—even though I was conversing as a Roman. Hopefully people got the gist in all the mess. But I knew what would be even worse than the pain: being marked down after that embarrassing incident.

We had been told as a year group that one person was going to be kicked out and several of us were on the chopping block. My hands were shaking as I stood outside the office of Aubrey Mellor, the head of the school at the time. I was devastated. I honestly believed I was going to be humiliated and kicked out. I didn't mean to come across as someone who was disaffected by what was being taught. I was genuinely disoriented and frustrated that no room was made for error in a space that was supposedly for learning. Deep down I knew I wasn't alone in this, but I felt like I couldn't share that with anyone in my year. As kind and generous as some of my classmates had been to me, I got the vibe that no one really wanted to get into a discussion about how difficult the course was. Especially when hundreds of people across the country auditioned to be where we were and would gladly take our place. So, I never wanted to imply that my worries or concerns were more than those of others. Thankfully, Aubrey told me I wasn't going to be kicked out—but I did have to 'make an effort'.

I wasn't going to let my dream slip away, so I began turning up half an hour before class every morning to warm up my voice, and I taught myself to code switch—slowly building that awareness of how I was communicating in each environment I found myself in. Not to mention the volume at which I spoke. We were so time poor that nothing else existed outside my class—especially my parents. Mum hated not hearing from me, even though I would be at school roughly twelve hours each day. In a moment of homesickness I broke down and called her and told her I wanted to quit. But that's not the way she raised me. She reminded me that I'd come this far, why give up now?

I would not have been able to get through those three years had it not been for the support of my family, especially my mum and dad. Relatives, particularly my Aunt Jenny and Uncle Bob, cooked food for me when I managed to catch the train out to the Sutherland Shire. My dad would help me edit my essays. My late Aunty Meryl, who was a very talented singer in amateur musicals, helping me with my singing voice. I miss hearing her sing 'Happy birthday' in an operatic voice at family celebrations.

Finding kindred spirits made me realise I wasn't as isolated as I had originally thought. As I was entering second year Shari Sebbens, another Top End girl, had been accepted into first year. I had heard about this young Bardi Jabirr-Jabirr woman from my mum. Shari's mother, Aunty Anna, was an Aboriginal and Islander Education Worker (AIEW) like mine, and the two of them had bonded over each of their daughter's passion for acting. Talking with her and her partner, Dale, made me feel like I had known them for years.

I was also thankful to meet Black creatives who were out in the big wide world making the art they wanted to see. Having the NIDA tutors introduce me to Leah Purcell and Wayne Blair while I was still studying kept the fire in me. If I genuinely wanted to be where they were, then I needed to carry the same resilience that got them there.

Then when I got to my third and final year, Wongutha-Yamatji man Meyne Wyatt and Birripi-Worimi man from La Perouse Guy Simon had secured places in first year. Even though we had all come from different parts of the country and had our own unique perspectives as artists there was an ease being around them because there was an implicit understanding between us. We all knew what it was like to be in the minority—even if we did get on with the others in class. I cannot express the level of relief and fortitude I felt not having to justify the way I saw the world or why I was there.

Over time I began to develop a thicker skin. It sucked to be the first person to perform, but I would often put my hand up anyway. I started to embrace failing because it meant I was learning and not playing it safe.

My third year was when another thing came full circle. Darren Gilshenan, who had played Truffaldino in *The Servant of Two Masters* when I did the Bell Shakespeare scholarship— was going to direct the very same play for our year at NIDA. I absolutely lost my mind. Maybe it was tenacity, maybe it was serendipity, maybe it was both—but how often does it happen to an actor that they get to perform in a play they watched when they were seventeen years old? I was completely in love with the character of Smeraldina, the lover of Truffaldino. She was so vivacious and sassy and I wanted nothing more than to play her. To my surprise, Darren gave me that part. I was overjoyed. Maybe I felt at ease in the role because I had loved the play so much as a teenager. Maybe Darren's enthusiasm for comedy was infectious. But he trusted me. He knew I could do it, so I began to believe I could, too. He reminded me that you're meant to have fun when you perform. It's not to say you completely forget your craft, because Darren was meticulous in his craft and expected the same of ours, but I was grateful that he had created a space where we could enjoy what we were all doing on stage.

Then, something happened that would change my life. The beautiful Ursula Yovich (who would later play my mother in *Top End Wedding*) had been cast in the title role of *Yibiyung* at Belvoir St Theatre, a prestigious theatre company in Sydney.

Written by Dallas Winmar, the play is based on Dallas's grandmother's journey back to her uncle, who was the father figure in her life. Similarly to the girls in *Rabbit-Proof Fence*, Yibiyung had been taken by authorities to the Moore River Native Settlement in Western Australia. Like Molly, Yibiyung uses the knowledge her uncle taught her to find her way back home. Ursula had fallen pregnant and the schedule for the Belvoir was too close to her due date, so she wasn't able to perform the role in Sydney. There wasn't a whole lot of time to recast, and it left it open for any young Aboriginal woman to be cast in her place. I'm so thankful to Ursula for putting my name forward, because the director, Wesley Enoch, called the head of acting at NIDA to ask if I could audition for the role. No one was allowed to take paid acting work while they were studying at NIDA, and they were understandably apprehensive about making an exception for me. But roles for Aboriginal women were sparse at this time, so if it came down to it, I would have pulled out of my degree. (Toni Collette famously pulled out of NIDA to take on a stage production of *Uncle Vanya* and then a part in the Anthony Hopkin's film *Spotswood* before she was cast in her breakout role in *Muriel's Wedding*. Mum kindly reminded me that I look nothing like Toni Collette, and *Muriel's Wedding* is a film that went all around the world, so it was a terrible example.) However, Belvoir moved heaven and earth to make sure I could do the play and still get my degree. Which was an unbelievable thing to happen to a drama student who still hadn't graduated. I should have felt guilty that this came along for me, but I knew that any of the actors in my year would have done the same. That role threw me into a completely different world from the institution I had been in for nearly three years. I was completely on my own. I had to take everything I had learned in those three years and put it into practice. With a piece that actually spoke to me.

I was thrown in the deep end, but my experiences at NIDA had made me resilient and quick-thinking. Obviously, I was very green next to the actors I shared the stage with. Not inferior, but new. You know what I mean. But my career has been built on being given opportunities I wasn't ready for. I'm a seasoned actor because of it.

I just want to say that even though my time at drama school was more awkward than my adolescence ever was, I would never deter young actors, particularly young Aboriginal actors, from applying to an acting school like NIDA. Yes, the lack of facilities in place to support Aboriginal and Torres Strait Islander students is disappointing. However, I have come to realise that this small industry in Australia does not know how to look after the wellbeing of its Aboriginal and Torres Strait Islander creatives. Unfortunately, the course is a reflection on the industry, especially when we are expected to relive issues we deal with in our daily lives on stage or in front of the camera.

For example, a few years after graduating from NIDA, I was cast in *The Secret River* at Sydney Theatre Company. Based on Kate Grenville's novel of the same name, it follows William Thornhill, an ex-convict who made himself at home along the Hawkesbury River in the late nineteenth century. Little did he know that the Traditional Owners, the Dharug people, dug for yams where he set up camp. Because he saw this family as a threat, he worked with the other convicts to kill them all. Even though I'm not Dharug, it shook me. These massacres happened all across this land. It was very draining to be brought into the world where Aboriginal people had to fight just to survive. I played a Dharug woman who was captured by Thornhill's neighbour, Smasher Sullivan, and chained up. I had a weird prosthetic mould that covered my breasts; in reality, though, it looked like breasts and I felt incredibly vulnerable—regardless of whether or not my real boobs were covered, I appeared to be topless. Even though the actor playing Smasher made sure I was comfortable and safe, I had to listen to his character tell William Thornhill how he had repeatedly raped the woman I was playing. Now, imagine performing that eight times a week for three months.

My training had built me up to be able to emotionally separate myself from this story after we finished performing every night. I felt incredibly unprofessional leaving my script in the rehearsal room each time, but the physical act of leaving the story there meant that mentally I wasn't taking it home with me. Performing in a show like this was a big ask for the Black artists who were in it. To relive that kind of trauma every night is emotionally and intellectually taxing, and not many non-Indigenous people working in theatre and film are aware of this impact. There were many untrained Aboriginal actors who were brilliant performers—but many of them didn't know what to do to look after themselves. Ursula was in the production at the time, so the onus fell on the two of us to check in with our castmates. We were happy to do it, but it wasn't our responsibility.

So, even though many people working in the industry believe that drama school isn't beneficial to promising young talent, I have been able to meet the demands of the industry because of it. And having the space to tell our stories is important to the cultural fabric of our country. Despite the opportunities I have been given, many artists and crew are expected to do a lot and be paid very little. Over my decade working as a professional actor, the Australian Government has continued to strip funding from the Arts, which of course has had a negative impact on the pay rates of all the hardworking artists and crew. Cutting costs means you don't have a lot of time to think about your craft—you're just getting through the shoot or rehearsals as quickly as possible to save money.

Our leaders treat drama and performance as if it is a hobby for us, as if it isn't important to reflect on who we are and to create empathy through understanding others. We don't have enough ridiculously wealthy people in Australia to act as philanthropists to fund our stories like in the United States, so the Arts do rely on Government funding to get things made. It's incredibly bureaucratic, but hey, why shouldn't it be part of Government spending to understand and help promote the importance of some introspection into who we are as a society? Especially when people around the world still think we live in corrugated-iron huts and ride kangaroos to get anywhere? Even though many in power don't see the relevance of it, cultural and creative enterprise gave $111.7 billion to Australia's economy in one year. Yes, believe it or not, Australians want to be entertained after a hard day at work, and they don't always want to watch something American or

British. But in a move that I find shocking, our current Prime Minister, Scott Morrison, and the Liberal/National Coalition, recently announced, without any consultation with the sector, the abolition of the Department of Communications and the Arts. Anything remotely creative now falls under a new department called the Department of Infrastructure, Transport, Regional Development and Communications. No Arts in the title and, it seems, no importance placed in what the Arts do. As this was happening, great swathes of our land were cloaked in smog because of the bushfires that were spreading rapidly across the country. During a drought. There was radio silence from many of our federal politicians and our PM headed off on holiday. It seems our priorities are completely out of whack.

So, as horrific things take place in this country, artists are stepping up to give back—performing to raise funds for bushfire victims and drought-affected communities. They are giving solace and putting a spotlight on often forgotten communities. But with no Arts Minister and no recognition of the benefit the Arts bring to Australians, they are being forced to think about what the next steps are. I don't know how I would be able to grasp the future of this industry if I didn't have my formal training behind me.

You might think I'm having one massive whinge, but I hope painting this picture for you will make you see that my training at NIDA has been one of the big reasons I have thrived. Drama school was beneficial for me personally because I reclaimed the tools I was given over those three years. I took the learnings that were useful to me, and dismissed the things that weren't. It helped me fathom the oftentimes thankless industry I was about to enter into. Graduating from NIDA was more than just a piece of paper for me—although I've noticed that I can be taken more seriously by some people when they discover I have a degree. Not every creative has to make art within the mainstream, but now I can decide whether I want to create within the structure or outside of it completely. In this country most artists have to do both.

I went from being a scared small-town girl to a confident young actor. My nerves will always be there, but I can now filter them into something productive because I know how to prepare for a role in a short amount of time. I have reached further than I ever thought possible because I adapted to my new environment. I was only going to get so far if I waited for others to tell me I was capable of doing the best job possible—so I eventually found that belief within myself. I managed to build an unshakable solidarity with many other

Black creatives, especially the ones who went through NIDA with me. They remind me that I'm not the only one who feels voiceless at times. Their courage and sense of humour keep my head above water.

Even if you don't want to be an actor, I hope that my story encourages you to manifest whatever is going to bring you happiness—no matter the roadblocks you encounter. Following my dreams meant making a lot of sacrifices, and I know that would be familiar to a lot of people who have chased their own dreams. Following your dreams always comes at a cost.

I'm sharing this with you because if a short, Aboriginal woman from the Northern Territory can do it, I have an inkling you can too.

CHAPTER FOUR

SHINE BRIGHT LIKE A ... SAPPHIRE

SOME ACTORS SPEND YEARS WAITING FOR THEIR BIG break. I'm incredibly grateful that mine came just a year and a half after I graduated from NIDA, when I saw the open audition for the film adaptation of the award-winning play *The Sapphires*, which was going to be directed by actor/director Wayne Blair. I couldn't believe it. It had been a play at Belvoir St Theatre five years before, when I was seventeen, and my mum had surprised me with tickets when we were in Sydney over the Christmas period. I had loved it and at this time I wanted nothing more than to be a Sapphire.

One of the biggest lessons I learned upon graduating was saving money. I had been told by one of the talented actors in *Yibiyung*, Russell Dykstra, that putting away money while you worked gave you some form of stability during the dreaded 'down time'. It would cover you for the most part while you prepared for auditions, stayed fit and kept up other skills such as writing, singing, dancing or playing an instrument. Yeah, you're totally expected to do all of that for free, which is why you need to love it. I know all of this sounds obvious to a lot of actors, but it was all new to me. I had my dream job! I was out in the big wide world, twenty-one and carefree. Budgeting, shmudgeting! You can't take it with you. Naturally, I was going to treat myself. A little too much. *Yibiyung* closed successfully, but Sydney rent was starting to climb, and I had not taken Russell's advice seriously.

I could no longer afford to live in Sydney but if I had gone back to Darwin to live with my parents it would be hard to be seen for auditions. Established actors get to live where they want but recently graduated actors needed to be in Sydney to attend auditions at a moment's notice. Thankfully, Aunty

Jenny and Uncle Bob put me up until I could find my feet, and my parents helped me out with money for food.

In the meantime, I looked for flexible work. I know I wasn't the first actor to line up at Centrelink to apply for Newstart but you're sure made to feel like a deadbeat.

I kept getting turned away from hospitality work because Sydney was big enough for cafe owners and hotel managers to have the luxury of being really picky with who they employed. McDonald's wasn't enough for them.

Aunty Jenny and Uncle Bob lived near a family of high-achievers called the Hitchcocks. Cynthia Hitchcock was originally from Saibai Island in the Torres Strait, and most of her children loved performing like me. Even if they hadn't gone on to pursue work in the performing arts, they were still musical and well read. Cynthia's daughter Xena had gone around with me as I was trying to find work so I wouldn't lose faith. We went to a Jamaica Blue cafe and the manager told me he had no work for me, but asked Xena (in front of me) what experience she had and if she was looking for work. Are you kidding me, dude? She's got work! Hello, talk to the person who came to you for work! This period in my life was another big learning curve for me. If I was going to keep acting, then I had to put money away whenever I earned it. Or, do what my careers advisor had told me back in high school, and find a plan B.

Despite my lack of frugality, I had begun to make a name for myself. I had established connections with Bell Shakespeare and Belvoir St Theatre. There were people out in the industry who knew how hungry I was. I was ambitious enough to know that when an opportunity came along, I would take it. So when I received an email regarding the open auditions for the film adaptation of *The Sapphires*, I got my agents onto it straightaway.

The Sapphires followed four sexy, quick-witted, audacious Aboriginal women who sang soul music to the American Troops during the Vietnam War. Three sisters, Gail, Cynthia and Julie and their cousin Kay had taken up this opportunity after months of their talent and industrious nature not being recognised in their own country.

Written by proud Yorta Yorta actor Tony Briggs, these women were loosely based on his mother Laurel Robinson and Aunties Naomi Mayers, Lois Peeler and Beverly Briggs, who had formed a girl group called The Sapphires in the late 60s. As well as being talented singers, their activism broke new ground for the wider Aboriginal community throughout Sydney and Melbourne. Aunty Naomi, Laurel and Beverly helped set up the Aboriginal Medical Service. Aunty Lois was the first Aboriginal model and went on to become principal at Worowa Aboriginal College. It's Aboriginal women like them who are the reason I'm afforded many of the freedoms I have today.

In the stage adaptation I saw, these four roles had been played by prominent actors who have graced Australian stage and screen: Rachael Maza, Deborah Mailman, Lisa Flanagan and Ursula Yovich. I truly believe that I would not have had the opportunities that have been granted to me had these women not been absolute bosses at their craft, paving the way for women like me. It made me want to be right up there with them. As an awkward drama nerd who had just graduated high school, it was definitely the thing I needed to see. I had never felt so empowered as a modern Aboriginal woman.

So, when the opportunity came along for the film, I *had* to be in it. After having chased my agent about it, I was told that the director, Wayne Blair, and casting agent, Nikki Barrett, wanted me to audition for the role of the middle sister, Cynthia. Cynthia was the wild child. After being left at the altar she decides to put herself out there, maybe hook up with a soldier and get her groove back.

Because they were looking at Black girls across the whole damn continent, it was going to take forever for them to find the four women they wanted. While I waited to hear back, I had managed to find work up in the NT with the Darwin Theatre Company's adaptation of *A Midsummer Night's Dream*. I was offered the role of the naughty fairy Puck. My sissy Shari was cast as one of the lovers Hermia. We had our director, Marcel Schmitz, and producer of the play, Sam Young, help us send tapes.

Months passed, and I began to lose my mind. I would rather be told as soon as possible that I didn't get the role, to have it ripped off like a band-aid. But it really is out of your control, so all you can do is be prepared for the audition so that you can leave the room knowing that you had given it your best shot. Shari and I had closed the season of *A Midsummer Night's Dream*, and gone back to the grind in Sydney. I got a call from my agent saying that they had liked the tape I sent and wanted me to audition in person. Shari had received the same call. I slept over at Shari and Dale's apartment before the first audition so we could go over our lines together. We were paired with lots of other Aboriginal women so they could see how our chemistry worked. I understood then. Wayne, Nikki and the producers at Goalpost needed to believe we could be sisters. I read books on the Vietnam War. Xena's sister Jessica has an incredible voice and she taught me how to sing like The Supremes and other Motown stars. The audition process ended up taking eight months. I tried not to get my hopes up, but it was too late. I had already made it life and death. Not healthy at all. I was at my aunty and uncle's place. I received a missed call from my agent. That was it. I didn't get it. I took a big deep breath, and told myself that more roles would come along. When I spoke to my agent, she was very level headed, so when she told me I got the part I was extremely confused. What did she say? Then when she repeated herself, I almost deafened her with my squeals of rapture. I ran up to my cousin and we hugged for a long time. I wouldn't have been able to survive in Sydney without the support of my family.

I didn't know who else had been cast and I didn't want to call Shari to find out over the phone. I flew back to Darwin for the weekend, and Shari happened to be there as well. We met up at Throb Nightclub, the only gay club in Darwin and the best place to party and dance. We were each hoping the other had got their role and we both screamed as we shared the news ... we were to be castmates. Once we stopped hugging and cheering for each other we took over the dance floor to celebrate.

The experience of working with Shari, Deborah Mailman and Jessica Mauboy was almost indescribable. It was one of those extraordinary ensembles that lifts everyone on set. It really was magic, and that magic continued as the movie achieved box office and critical success. It was a very awe-inspiring thing for a young actor to be involved in.

Six months after we wrapped the film I received the call from the producer Rosemary Blight to share some amazing news: *The Sapphires* had been accepted into the Cannes Film Festival. I could not believe that the very first film I had acted in was going to be screened at the same prestigious festival as *Priscilla, Queen of the Desert* had been in 1994. I was on the phone to my parents straightaway. I had to stop my mum from booking flights then and there, because an event of this calibre didn't give out tickets to just anyone, not even my mum. But she was desperate to come, and said that if need be she and my dad would stand outside, behind the fence and wave as I walked into the screening at the Palais.

I couldn't think of a sadder image than my parents trying to call out to me from a busy crowd as if they were complete strangers, so I begged Rosemary to see if she could get a couple of extra tickets. My dad was about to turn sixty and, like me, he had never been to Europe, and I couldn't imagine a better way to spend his special birthday than to come to see his daughter at the Cannes Film Festival.

A few days later, Rosemary called to tell me that my parents had tickets to the screening. I couldn't thank her enough. Now came the scramble to get bags packed and red-carpet dresses ready for the flight two weeks later. Before I knew it I was in the back of a fancy car on our way from Nice airport getting lectured by the French driver about how to pronounce Cannes correctly: like *can* of beans, not *Cairns*. 'There is no *s*!' he sniffed, but not even he could dampen my mood. What a way to come to Europe for the first time!

Shari, Deb, Jess and I were invited to a Screen Australia function, where there was a ceiling-to-floor poster of *The Sapphires*. The view of the Mediterranean from the high-rise office was spectacular. Someone pointed to what looked like a navy vessel and told us it was P Diddy's boat. I have no idea what P Diddy was promoting in the south of France, but I guess if you have an ocean liner to yourself you can do whatever you damn well please. Apparently Eva Longoria had brought a boat over, too. This kind of opulence was a world away from Kakadu.

We all met in the foyer of a fancy hotel and then we got into a limo for the great two-minute journey down the road to the red carpet. I realise this is how it all works; the glamour of film. We get into a car so we can get out of it. The song 'Soul Man' came on as we went up to the steps of the theatre and we couldn't help but dance! It probably wasn't the done thing but, hey, it's not as if they were not going to play the film after that. It's widely known that more than any other festival, the people who attend Cannes are passionately vocal about film. They will either love what you've done or hate it—there is no in between. There will be no ambivalence—they will make their feelings known either way. Naturally, that made me feel particularly nervous, but when the credits came up, the crowd lifted to applause and continued through a ten-minute standing ovation. I was thrilled. There was a guy walking around with a camera and the video fed onto the screen. It went to Wayne first, then to Deborah Mailman, Shari Sebbens, Jessica Mauboy and me. They took the time to congratulate each individual for their contribution to the work, which I was very touched by. When I came out of the theatre Mum and Dad were wiping tears away from their eyes and all Mum could say through her sobs was, 'I was fine until your father started.'

To go from Darwin to Cannes was beyond anything I had imagined. The *Hollywood Reporter* said this: 'a sparkling charmer ... about four spunky indigenous [sic] women whose powerhouse voices catapulted them onto the sixties-era world stage as Australia's answer to the Supremes'. *Rolling Stone* called the movie 'a blast of joy and music that struts right into your heart'.

The Sapphires will always be in my heart, and the role gifted me many opportunities. I have managed to work consistently as an actor in a very small industry ever since. After the film I travelled around the continent working on a short film in Alice Springs, a telemovie in regional Queensland, and a play that toured in Sydney and Perth. No one could say I was green anymore, because I had all of this behind me—and I was only twenty-four.

Just when I was planning for things to dry up, the audition for the Channel 9 show *Love Child* came along. The story followed Joan Miller, a midwife who had just taken up residency at Stanton House, a ward for unmarried expectant mothers. Set in 1969, the show resonated with many Aboriginal and non-Aboriginal people who either had babies snatched out of their arms or had suffered displacement as a result of being removed as a baby. I was auditioning for the role of Martha, one of the Stanton House girls and a member of the Stolen Generation. Taken from her family as a toddler, Martha had fallen pregnant after being raped by the man she worked for. Martha shared the resilience many Aboriginal women needed to survive this terrible trauma.

I had to learn a very heartwarming scene in which Martha and the other girls from Stanton House, Viv and Patty, sneak out of the accommodation (they're on strict orders to not leave the grounds) and they buy and share Italian pastries. I love a good prop, so as I was on my way to the audition I bought pastries to eat in the scene. After *The Sapphires*, I learned how to deliver a one-liner without trying to be funny—and Martha had some great one-liners.

A few weeks later I went to Darwin to visit my parents and relatives up home. They had taken me out bush, where we used to camp. We were drinking tea on the beach when my agent called to say I got the part. Thank you, Telstra.

While Martha isn't based on anyone in particular, it was a massive responsibility to be the only actor in a prime-time show to represent a whole group of Aboriginal people who had been ripped from their families. This is an incredible responsibility and challenge. It also meant it was incumbent on me to speak up when things weren't right, which is never easy and certainly never fun. But with a bit more experience under my belt, I felt more confident when I had to bring up occasional issues. I'd learned how to phrase things in a way that no one felt their toes being stepped on but still got the results needed to make a character that felt authentic.

We had to film the scene in which Martha goes into labour. While I had a kind and thoughtful director, it was strange being directed by a man during all the pretend screams and moans of pain. Like, I know he would have been there for his wife giving birth, but not having given birth myself, I guess I was hoping to be guided by someone whose body had actually gone through the process of labour. I was touched to see that I had made a few women in the crew cry. I must have done something right.

It wasn't the first time I had played a pregnant woman. Not long after *The Sapphires*, Warwick Thornton had cast me in his film *True Gods*, which was a part of an anthology of short films called *Words with Gods*. I played a heavily pregnant woman who had driven out to the desert, out to country to find the strength and certainty she needed for this new phase of her life. Like her ancestors before her, she gives birth under a tree. I don't know why people like seeing me with a swollen belly but I've been told it suits me.

But that doesn't make it any less embarrassing. As Martha, I had fifty people around me trying to create the illusion of an actual labour, so they're watching me screaming with my legs open. While lights and cameras were being set up, there was an actor who wanted to talk about the kind of gloves he was wearing—and while I get on with him, in that moment I truly wanted to throttle him. Gloves were not the priority of the scene.

The adorable Black baby I was meant to hold was only a week old, and the dad, an Aboriginal fella who would have only been shy of twenty, was clearly freaking out about other people holding his newborn son. I could also sense he and his girlfriend were feeling very out of place and everyone on set was too distracted to reassure them. When I managed to get eye contact with him, I smiled, gave a nod and said, 'Hey brother, thanks for letting me hold Bub. He's beautiful.' Then I sang 'Ngarra Burra Ferra' to the baby, the Yorta Yorta song that the Sapphire girls sang. Bub stopped crying.

A few weeks after I wrapped the first season of *Love Child*, I was asked by NIDA to help run a unique workshop where the recipients had a week to create a short film. It was organised and backed by Baz Luhrmann and Samsung, and the short film was going to be screened at the Sydney Opera House a few weeks after. Many alumni return to NIDA to teach the short courses, which I had been doing on and off between acting gigs. I found it a valuable thing to be able to articulate what you do as an actor, because you gain a stronger understanding of what you do to get into a role and how you do it.

There were mentors for directing, writing and acting. I was there to mentor the handful of actors who had been selected. Luckily, the screenwriting mentor, Josh Tyler, was a trained actor as well, so he was able to help me with a larger group. He had just finished writing a TV mockumentary series called *Plonk*, which followed comedian Chris Taylor from *The Chaser* as a heightened version of himself wine tasting at vineyards across Australia. I had a great little cackle watching the show on YouTube after he told me about it when we met. I noticed that, like many writers can be, while he was a great conversationalist, Josh was still reserved. That being said, it was very easy for us to make each other laugh. Which was a blessing because teaching can be very demanding.

Across the fortnight of this workshop, we referenced films constantly to talk about scenes that worked or didn't. Josh and I would often hang out in the breaks and talk about our favourite films, and we soon realised we were mostly talking about romantic comedies. *When Harry Met Sally, Sleepless in Seattle, Notting Hill, Four Weddings and A Funeral.* The classics.

When I told Josh I was born in the Northern Territory, he spoke about his own fond memories of being up there with his wife, Tahli. Not many people I meet in Sydney have been to the Territory, so it was refreshing to go beyond talking about how expensive it is to fly up there. It was lovely to be able to describe how special it was for me to grow up there—feeling like Simba from *The Lion King* on top of ancient sandstone escarpments overlooking luscious green floodplains, chasing waterfalls, not sticking to the rivers and lakes like I'm used to.

One day Josh said in a break: 'Hey, when we have lunch, do you want to have a chat? I just want to talk to you about something.' He seemed very serious, and I thought he was going to be frank with me about my shortcomings as a teacher.

We were in the foyer of Carriageworks in our lunch break when Josh told me that all our talk of the Territory and rom-coms had sparked an idea: he thought we should set one up there.

Let's just let that settle a moment. *We should set one up there.* What?!

I was blown away by this idea. I had given up writing plays and screenplays—to paraphrase Ta-Nehisi Coates, my best thoughts never managed to translate when I put them on paper. But here was someone who believed I could do more than act or teach acting—someone who thought I could write and make a film. That was an amazing thing. Having someone believe you can do something can often be the nudge you need to believe in yourself. I already knew I had something to say; all I had to do now was push past my doubts and trust in my abilities in order to say it.

CHAPTER FIVE

MAKING THINGS CHANGE

O N SUNDAY, 3 MAY 2015 I WAS FORTUNATE ENOUGH TO win two awards at the Logie Awards, a popular television awards event in Australia. I had been nominated for my role as Martha in *Love Child*. I had taken my obligation to Martha's story very seriously and when I found out I had been nominated, that pressure inspired me to prepare and write an acceptance speech. I knew that if I won and was given the opportunity to say something I had to take it, because it might not happen again.

It was an exciting time to be an Aboriginal actor, because more and more Aboriginal producers and writers were creating stories for Aboriginal and Torres Strait Islanders to lead in. Groundbreaking shows such as *Redfern Now, Black Comedy, The Gods of Wheat Street* and *8MMM* had gone to air and people wanted more. *Cleverman* was about to go into production.

Earlier that year, April Reign's #OscarsSoWhite hashtag had begun a massive conversation on social media about the kinds of artists and stories that are valued in Hollywood. It was from seeing the tweets that came of that, that I was able to find my own language to paint a picture of the lack of imagination in our local industry: from which stories in Australia gain recognition, to the writing and casting of people of colour in Australian stories.

The character of Martha in *Love Child* was an important one, because she was an Aboriginal lead character on prime-time television who was sharing a poignant reality about young women in the 1960s, and especially about young Aboriginal women. I was very proud of the work I had done to research her and the way I had worked with the creatives on the set to give her the authenticity that was needed.

That night was very special for me. I was a young Black actor finding my way, and to hear my name called was incredible. I had a microphone and I owed it to every other person of colour to make the most of it. In my speech I spoke from my heart about putting 'more beautiful people of colour on TV and connect viewers in ways which transcend race and unite us'.

My words were met with resounding applause. Actors, producers, writers and directors seemed excited by the conversation my speech had ignited. Many actors before me—Justine Saunders, Bob Maza, Deborah Mailman, Aaron Pedersen, Shari Sebbens to name a few—had brought up the lack of representation long before I was in the industry. In my naïvety I honestly believed that people had spoken up on the subject so that the people who had to make conscious decisions about who was in front of and behind the camera, might truly open up the space. After all, aren't we supposed to be the ones holding up the mirror to our society?

I'm not as naïve now. Five years have gone by and we are still discussing how casting can be more conscious and inclusive. Nearly every journalist asks me, 'Do you believe things have changed?' The statistics tell us they haven't. In the most recent industry drama report, eighty-three per cent of the leading roles and recurring characters are played by actors of Anglo-Saxon and Celtic backgrounds. But you just have to look at mainstream television to know that it's actually going backwards. Believe me, I don't enjoy having this constant exchange with my fellow artists. To depict race, gender, sexuality and disability with the respect it deserves in Australian storytelling is not fun banter for me. But until performers who represent the majority on screen go in to bat for equal representation, things will not change. I think it's fair to say that Geraldine Viswanathan, Remy Hii, Chris Pang and Aisha Dee had to chase success in Hollywood because no one back in Australia had the ingenuity to reflect what the public really looks like. Quite frankly it's gutless of the industry to not have more people of colour behind the camera as well, so that the collaboration of a project is richer, more honest and more authentic.

I have never understood why some non-Indigenous creatives see diversity as a block to their creativity. I believe it's a weak excuse to be told that it's a token gesture to write a person of colour into your script. You lack originality and enterprise if you erase the people who live in the world—regardless of whether they live in your street. Also, judge me all you want, but I love pop culture. My favourite conversations with family and friends have been over the books they couldn't put down, the TV shows they binged on until 2am and the films they've loved or loathed. But a lot of the things I read, see and hear are speaking from a different place from where I've been. I know I'm not the only brown girl to have spent a shit-tonne of my hard-earned money on things that don't speak to me. If we can believe in crazy ideas like a game called Quidditch or a throne that a fire-breathing dragon melted—it shouldn't be a big stretch of the imagination that someone who lives differently from you exists in your kitchen sink drama.

I mean, for goodness sake, I'm not asking for every character I play to bring up the Northern Territory intervention or the fact that Indigenous people in this country make up twenty-three per cent of the prison population, or that the life-expectancy gap between a non-Aboriginal and First Nations person is twenty years. What I am asking is to celebrate modern Aboriginal culture, to subvert the stereotypes that have been pitted against Aboriginal people—that we don't believe in hard work, that we're negligent with our children, that we're all criminals or that we all have alcohol problems. To instead show the complexity and commonplace that we all share while also acknowledging the uniqueness of our story.

When I went to drama school, the general consensus was that the epitome of storytelling came from Anglo-Saxon stories from Britain and the United States. It is taking a lot of effort to shift that entrenched belief.

I'm very inspired by exciting romantic comedies that people of colour are making around the world. *The Big Sick, Crazy Rich Asians, The Incredible Jessica James* and *Ali's Wedding* are all examples of great storytelling that breaks down clichés and stereotypes. If you were to ask me to list my top favourite feature films, they would be it. Watching these films made me realise how much rom-coms can remind the audience of each other's humanity. When done well, romantic comedy can be as provocative as drama. Every human around the world understands love and loss, which is why people keep coming back to this genre. This implicit understanding means that the characters don't have to have European lineage to understand the ups and downs of being in love. Even though I don't belong to any of the communities depicted in these films, it was heartwarming to be invited inside a world that wasn't mine. Also, none of the female protagonists had to compromise their happiness for the sake of being in a heteronormative relationship. These films were speaking to people who have been sidelined in Western storytelling for so long, despite existing and thriving in the Western world for much longer.

While it's disappointing to hear that talented performers like Remy, Chris and Ronny Chieng had to leave Australia to find work, it made me very happy to see three men from Australia in the hit film of 2018. Sure, it might have been about rich people, but don't Chinese people around the world deserve fairytales just like anyone else? When talking about Sandra Oh being the first woman of Asian heritage to be nominated for an Emmy for Best Female Actor in a Leading Role for the series *Killing Eve*, the star of *Crazy Rich Asians*, Constance Wu says, 'I think that says something about who the culture thinks has a story that's worth telling.'

Films like *Crazy Rich Asians* prove that stories involving a cast that isn't Anglo-Saxon can speak to a broad audience. And to have people of colour making rom-coms makes my heart want to burst. If you have not seen *The Big Sick*, quit messing around and put it on right now. In *Time* magazine, Kumail Nanjiani talks about how co-writing *The Big Sick* with his wife, Emily V Gordon, helped make his experience as a Pakistani–American man more relevant to wider America. The couple wanted the film to show that his family, the way he lived and fell in love were more universal than people once believed it to be. I didn't need to be Pakistani to love how concerned his family were, be upset with how heartbroken the character

Emily was, and feel sorry for how discombobulated Kumail's character felt. They told this story, with all the magic of love and cheekiness. Kumail's wealthy knowledge of rom-coms meant that he saw the potential in making his identity accessible to a broader audience because the genre is well known for saying something deeper. 'The best ones are always about something more than just the couple getting together. *Sleepless in Seattle* is about grieving. *When Harry Met Sally* is about people getting to know each other over decades. 'People don't want escapist, mindless entertainment right now,' Nanjiani says. 'People want stuff that really speaks to something.'

I adore the fact that people of colour are beginning to write and produce their own versions of the genre. A slight weight was lifted off my shoulders because they were people I could relate to—not apologising for who they were, rather they were being the hero of their own story. Hugh Grant is gorgeous but he doesn't represent them. They make me grin from ear to ear long after their films have ended. So often when an actor who isn't Caucasian is cast in a rom-com, they're just there to facilitate what the blonde-haired, blue-eyed lead desires. But whether they set out to do it or not, performers such as Kumail, Jessica Williams and Constance Wu make someone like me believe that I too deserve the fairytale.

When Kumail and Emily were writing *The Big Sick*, they understood the significance of normalising a Muslim family living in America, showing an honest depiction as a 'happy side effect' to the story. 'My in-laws are always speaking Urdu,' Emily told *Time*. 'I've never seen that in a movie or a TV show that wasn't them planning something nefarious.'

When Josh planted the idea of writing a film together, these films were my inspiration. As much as I wish I didn't have to justify or validate my lived experience on a daily basis, the Australian media's all-too-common degrading rhetoric about Aboriginal people leaves me no choice. Humanity is brought back to Aboriginal people when they see themselves reflected on screens in all their complexity. And that humanity is translated to everyone watching. Not only do their lives seem less alien to the wider mainstream audience it also strengthens the love they have for themselves and their community. It makes them feel like their perspectives on Australian society and history matter. It should matter to people who aren't Indigenous to this land. The only way the majority of Australians will feel empathetic enough to change the system that favours them is if they regularly put themselves in the shoes of marginalised people. Many won't have the capacity to do that if marginalised creatives and stories sit on the fringes of modern Australian storytelling. The stories I create might not improve the awful things that continue to oppress Aboriginal people, but if even a small number of non-Indigenous people in an audience can believe that the general wellbeing and safety of Aboriginal and Torres Strait Islanders should be prioritised to the same degree as non-Indigenous lives, then I've done my job.

As a Black woman with a profile I feel I have to speak up, I have to push for some form of substantive change. Making one speech was not enough; I had to follow through, I wanted to take my anguish over how stagnant the conversation had become about diversity and begin writing the things I wanted to see at the cinema. I realised very quickly that the mind-blowing experience I had with *The Sapphires* was a magical one-off thing—that I couldn't simply wait for someone to give me that experience again.

For me, it's more than just giving Aboriginal people and other minorities opportunities to further their craft, which of course is incredibly important. It's also about stories dismantling the narrative that Australia has curated about Aboriginal people for so long. Particularly about Aboriginal women. Sometimes, I can kid myself that we have come a long way and that it is better. But then I see a cartoon of Serena

Williams or a video clip of a famous stand-up comedian denigrating a woman of colour to an audience raucously laughing and I know it is not. I wrote this book so that I don't have to repeat myself time and time again. The way women of colour continue to be portrayed in the media is pure laziness by the people who write about them.

I recently read a book called *Skin Deep* by Liz Conor, which uncovers some sobering accounts about the way settlers from the United Kingdom defined Aboriginal women across the eighteenth, nineteenth and twentieth centuries. Conor collated all of these accounts to point out how settlers tried to rationalise cruel, unjust and violent exercises of power against First Nations women by minstrelising the way that they looked. I'm not talking about blackface—which is a huge part of that—I'm specifically talking about writing over-exaggerated details of their facial features and body parts to point out how different they were, how 'inhuman' they were. Let's just say Anglo-Saxons were the ones who pointed out the difference first, so I have no time for all the 'humanists' who believe that people of colour are the ones who point out difference. A statement that really struck me was: 'appearance was a means to enact racialised power, capable of withholding cultural presence and legitimacy'.

But that's how far these stereotypes go back. The heart of the book encapsulated the concept that the more un-human Aboriginal women seemed to the coloniser's eye, the more power they could hold over them.

If ever we needed to see a modern interpretation of this, you only have to look at Mark Knight's cartoon of Serena Williams that appeared in the *Herald-Sun*. This was about putting a woman of colour in her place and scolding her for speaking up. How were young girls of colour supposed to interpret this?

However, it also made me think about all the people this doesn't affect, how a lot of them would be doing things like drinking rosé or watching *Ozark* on Netflix while I read *Skin Deep*. You know what? Real change will come when more non-Aboriginal people crack a history book like *Skin Deep* and I can finally drink that rosé and watch *Ozark* instead. Quite frankly I'd love a damn break from what I already know.

There are too many instances across the last decade where the appearance of an Australian Indigenous woman has been brought to international attention in a negative way. No wonder so many of my Aboriginal girlfriends get fetishised or rejected harshly on Tinder.

On 17 February 2015, an episode of the US sitcom *2 Broke Girls*, starring Kat Dennings and Beth Behrs, featured an episode in which their boss, Han, whose sole premise is to make people laugh at his thick Asian accent, enters distressed that he can't find his iPad. 'I've been having a casual flirtation with a woman from Australia. She is part Aboriginal, but she has a great personality.'

Now I know this guy is a hack. I mean, why deliver a funny shooting script when there's *World of Warcraft* to be played? But don't worry ladies, I'm sure he has a great personality.

A couple of days after that aired, and after a fierce backlash, Kat Dennings tweeted: 'That line was a moment of ignorance from whoever wrote it. It does NOT reflect how I or the cast feels. Hope this helps anyone rightfully upset.'

It didn't, but hers was a much better response than that of the show's creator Michael King, who has previously clapped back at allegations of the show making racist stereotypes by saying, 'I'm gay. I put in gay stereotypes every week! I don't find it offensive … I find it comic to take everybody down, which is what we are doing.'

Listen Michael, the world has never been an even playing field, and you are not helpful to anyone kicking down other minorities.

Maybe Michael King was riffing off comedian and host of *The Daily Show* Trevor Noah's 2013 stand-up show. I will never know how Noah, a South African man of colour, could think it was funny to say: 'All women of every race can be beautiful. I bet some of you sitting there now are saying, "Oh but Trevor I haven't met a beautiful Aborigine." But you know what you say? You say *yet*. You haven't met a beautiful Aborigine *yet*. Coz you haven't seen all of them, right? And also, it's not always about looks. Maybe Aborigin[al] women do special things. Maybe they just jump on top of you and be like [pretends to perform fellacio like playing a didgeridoo].' The video went viral around Australia in 2017, and many Aboriginal people around the country were hurt by what they heard.

Friends begged me not to watch the clip, but it was about women like me. I had to know what was being said about me and the women I love so much.

Even though I had mentally prepared myself, my eyes still stung from tears of anger, my face burned, I sweated, my heart raced.

As much as I don't want to let these stupid things get to me, I work so hard to change all of these perceptions people make about Aboriginal and Torres Strait Islander women, and I feel as if I go two steps back whenever this happens. It leaves me infuriated and exhausted. It's boring to take people through why it's offensive.

I have written this book so that if people want to know why I take this stuff so personally, I can say, 'Read my book' and walk away.

The way I have lived and the way the world perceives women like me is not an idea you can just toss up in the air and see where it lands without my sisters and me setting the record straight.

Although Noah removed the video from YouTube, the damage had already been done. He'd reinforced a stereotype by riffing on an age-old (and totally wrong) joke of Aboriginal women being ugly yet hypersexual and simple-minded. It made me sick to think that he was telling all these people across the world, who probably have never met an Aboriginal woman, that a woman like me would give my body over freely to anyone because I'm too dumb to know what's happening to me.

He possibly felt that taking the video down was enough to make amends with my community. Most Aboriginal women would have forgiven him if he had made a meaningful apology, but he mentioned on multiple media platforms in Australia that he didn't feel he had to apologise for what he said in a routine he performed five years before. And the majority of viewers, particularly Anglo-Saxons, aren't going to look at how long ago it was and think, 'Gee, that's an old take. Aboriginal women must be gorgeous now.'

I'm sure he didn't want it to be the 'thing' that overshadowed his Australian tour, but ugliness like this needs to be called out and at the very least you hope the instigator learns and goes on to help counter what they put out there. Not Noah.

'I do understand how outrage works … people generally don't want to listen or understand from their side. They go no, we're angry. So all you can do is fall back and say, "Hey, I've addressed this,"' he said.

So, in the end, his feelings mattered more than any of the women he had trodden on. Saying sorry doesn't take away your responsibility. It means you need to work harder to make amends.

But the way any Aboriginal woman thinks or feels should never be so quickly dismissed. It's not easy to get someone to take responsibility for what they have said or done against Aboriginal women. Even when I've pulled someone up on saying something racist or sexist, they try to distract me by asking what it was about the comment that made it so.

I noticed when watching the clip that most of the audience in the front row were not brown like Noah. They were Caucasian. They were laughing, clapping and slapping their thighs like they knew exactly what he was talking about. There were no Australian Aboriginal women present in the audience that I could see, which made me wonder who his jokes were for. They definitely weren't for someone like me, since I'm part of the group he was punching down on. Being a Black South African man, he would have to understand how colonisation affects other Black and Indigenous groups.

He had to be aware that his audience was mostly White and how they perceived his Aboriginal Australian sisters. He chose us because he knew his audience didn't know enough about us to challenge it.

While Trevor Noah sits comfortably in his apartment in New York, Aboriginal women like me have to live with the reverberations of his words. The audience looks to comedians for 'truthful' observations about the world around them. They laugh when they acknowledge a gag they believe to be true. This 'joke' waters a seed already planted in racist minds, further cementing for them that we will always be less.

In 1979, five years before Trevor Noah was born, Serbian performance artist Marina Abramovic came to Australia and spent time with the Pitjantjatjara and Pintupi tribes of the Great Victorian Desert. Her autobiography, *Walk Through Walls: A Memoir*, had not yet been published when New York–

based art critic Rachel Wetzler shared a photo of an excerpt. The following is a diary entry from Abramovic's time in Australia.

> Aborigines are not just the oldest race in Australia; they are the oldest race on the planet. They look like dinosaurs. But at the same time, when you first meet them, you have to put effort into it. For one thing, to Western eyes they look terrible. Their faces are like no other faces on earth; they have big torsos (just one bad result of their encounter with Western civilisation is a high sugar diet that bloats their bodies) and sticklike legs.

Here was a woman who went on to make her name by staring into the eyes of someone to show her soul and reveal her depths and interpret those of the person looking back. Yet, she too failed to see a beauty other than a White version of feminine. Knight, King, Abramovic and Noah don't have to deconstruct their ideas, but every Aboriginal woman has to when they are told that they are quite attractive for someone who is Aboriginal.

The reason these comments cut so close to the bone for me is because I live with their consequences every day. But

I am lucky, because of where I am in my life I can push them aside most of the time. Many of my sisters can't. Women like Samantha Cooper—a case manager working in Queensland's Moreton Bay region who was sacked from her job two days after she filed an official complaint about micro-aggressive comments relating to her Aboriginality to the workplace watchdog.

Samantha was running a pilot program called 'Breaking Down the Barriers', which was designed to assist Aboriginal and Torres Strait Islander families through the Government-funded domestic violence organisation she worked for. During her time in the program, Samantha had been described as going 'walkabout', told she was 'quite pretty for an Aboriginal' and asked if she had ever met a 'real' Aboriginal person. Six months went by and after several attempts to address these comments more informally with her colleagues, she was left with no choice but to put forward the complaint.

The organisation in question claimed that funding cuts meant the program was no longer going to exist. However, a spokesperson for the Department of Child Safety, Youth and Women refuted that funding had been cut to Ms Cooper's program.

Samantha Cooper's story is one of many, and it's comments like Trevor Noah's that tell non-Indigenous people that it's okay to talk to and about Aboriginal women like that. That is the reason behind my hurt. It's crazy to me that Trevor Noah thinks that his platform and his words don't have power, that they don't influence the people who listen to him. It's insane that comedians like him claim that when people pull them up for being irresponsible, they are being censored. We are simply asking comedians to take responsibility for what they say.

The truth is, Aboriginal women don't need to be kicked down more than we already have been. Aboriginal and Torres Strait Islander women are thirty-seven times more likely to be hospitalised than non-Aboriginal women for non-fatal domestic violence related assaults. If people like Michael King, Trevor Noah, Mark Knight et al didn't help rob us of our humanity, this wouldn't happen to us.

How do we change that? How do we rewrite the story? It starts with telling the *whole* story. It starts with equal representation. It starts with having tough conversations. It starts with respect. Believe me, if non-Indigenous people are tired of hearing about diversity and representation, imagine how exhausting it is for people like me to speak about it. I've trawled through websites and libraries to ground my feelings and beliefs, so that people who hold power don't try to dismiss them. So, I am using my power and my voice to talk about the things that matter, to point out disrespect and to tell everyone with a platform to be wary of what that platform communicates.

Films such as *Muriel's Wedding* and *Priscilla, Queen of the Desert* surprised American audiences because they had something unique to say about Australia. I want that same reaction.

This is my shout out to fellow creatives to do better.

Acting schools—do better at considering who you give opportunity to. Do the next Margot Robbie and Hemsworth boys take up ninety per cent of your selection? There's plenty of them in Australia and Hollywood. I'm sure these students will work just as hard as I do, but honestly most can thrive in LA without the leg-up. If students of European descent are the only ones rocking up to auditions, that perhaps means they're the only students who can afford your training. Create programs to make your courses more accessible to passionate students who don't have financial or emotional support behind them. It's your job to facilitate that. If you already have them, make them more widely known.

Australian writers, creators and producers—what is it that you want to say about your country? How do you want it to be seen? It's all very well and good to be upset at the way Hollywood actors attempt the Australian accent, but what have you given them to reference? I get that Americans can live in their own bubble, but a lot of Australians are happy to play along with whatever they believe us to be. As good as Vegemite and Tim Tams are, is that all we eat? Do we only murder, rape or contend with animals that can kill us? How many Ned Kelly films do we need to make? How many times must I watch films following White people feeling guilty? I can say all this because I was named after Miranda in *Picnic At Hanging Rock*.

And finally, to the young Black dreamers who want to become actors—don't let anyone tell you that drama school is not for you. When I was studying I might have struggled at first and only learned about European art that I would never be cast in, yet it is because of these learnings that I found my place and can now deconstruct at length why these stories aren't relevant to me. My acting was very wooden when I first graduated, it took time to develop my skills. But I have tools to navigate this demanding industry. The raw 'gut instinct' that people believed I would lose comes back to me the more confident I am in a role. So, research the training institutions across the country and decide from there what you want. But remember, knowledge is power.

Despite knowing all this, or maybe because of it, I realised that no one was going to make the kind of stories that I wanted to see on screen, so I decided I was going to make them my damn self.

CHAPTER SIX

TOP END WEDDING

ONCE JOSH STARTED ME THINKING ABOUT FILM-making, I had to give myself permission to do it. I was keen to create Australian stories that had something more to say about the times we are living in. The serendipity of connecting with Josh over those few weeks was not lost on me either. Sometimes opportunities come along, and people come into your life and you have to be brave enough to follow them. I was going to be brave. I didn't want to wait years to see another film like *The Sapphires*. Aboriginal and Torres Strait Islanders deserve to watch more empowering and joyous films about themselves in mainstream media, and I was going to follow through on what I had called for in my Logies speech and make that happen.

I talked about this with Josh and fired up about the importance of representation in art. I also wanted people to realise that not only is the Northern Territory a beautiful place, but there is much more to the people who live there than clichéd portrayals allow us to realise. Josh listened and agreed and was ready to go on this journey with me.

But where to begin?

How do you actually get a film made? I knew how to write a script, how to act it out, I had a basic idea of direction and cinematography but the business side of things was a mystery to me. Luckily, Josh had a bit of experience there. We talked a lot about what we could do, our love of rom-coms and my love of the Top End—and gradually the idea for *Top End Wedding* was born. Josh wanted to make the bride-to-be from the Territory. He suggested that we could heighten the comedy like in *Meet the Parents*—where she brings her fella back home to meet her family and they just can't stand her fiancé. I also liked it in *My Big Fat Greek Wedding* where the groom-to-be is a complete stranger to the world he's brought into.

If you are a filmmaker or writer you'll understand how many versions you try before you find what sings. We sang quite a few versions of the song before Josh went away and worked up the first draft of a script for a trailer we thought we could shoot once we found money. It is a weird thing, but to make the movie we needed people to buy into the idea and to do that best we needed to make … a film! As Josh and I worked through the logistics I started to gain an idea of the behind-the-scenes complexities. We met with a producer, Glen Condie, to discuss finding the money for the mock-trailer for *Top End Wedding*. Glen was excited about the film and came on board. He stressed that there would be a greater chance that producers and distributors would visualise the story we wanted to tell (it can be a bit hard for them to picture when they're just reading a script) and buy in, so we all agreed the show reel had to be great.

While this was all happening, I had to keep working. Luckily, *Love Child* came back for season two. I was so happy that the producers had brought Leah Purcell on board in season two to not only assist with Martha's storyline, but to play Martha's estranged mother. Leah Purcell is Australian acting royalty. She is an award-winning actor, playwright, author, producer and proud Goa-Gunggari-Wakkawakka Murri woman from Queensland. Although we had some incredible writers on *Love Child*, I had been concerned in season one that there were no Aboriginal people in the writers' room. Because no one else on set had lived with this part of history behind them, they couldn't know how to articulate— even if they were well read or empathetic to the issues that stemmed from the Stolen Generation–Indigenous experience. Therefore, as I mentioned earlier, it was up to me to speak up if my gut told me something wasn't right.

Working on *Love Child* was the first time I ever really experienced the pace of commercial television. I would want to ask questions on set, particularly about how honestly we were portraying the time and the Aboriginal women affected by the circumstances, but sometimes the speed of the shoot prohibited further exploration. I knew that everyone was doing the best they could but I worried about what my community would think. Before this I had been fortunate enough to work on projects that had Aboriginal and Torres Strait Islanders at the helm, but this was different. No one really wanted an actor to talk about the writing when we were all working against an ambitious schedule. I was called a 'space cadet' often because I just struggled to be present on set. I had so many thoughts as I worked through some of the tougher scenes. I had to keep impostor syndrome at bay, I had to keep assuring myself that I deserved a place there. So, I just tried to become as dependable as I could and prove myself.

By the time I was given a script it would be too late to change anything. It was nerve-wracking thinking about my community watching. Would they be disappointed in the lack of representation? Did they see themselves or any of their family in this show? Not only that, we were working with so many babies, who were all gorgeous but unpredictable. Having Leah on board for season two made me feel like some weight had been taken off my shoulders. Leah had the experience, the knowledge and the respect to be listened to if something wasn't right.

It was because of Leah that my character, Martha, wasn't just fading into the woodwork. It had been incredibly ambitious of a commercial network to even make a show around unmarried mothers in the 60s, but I felt that everyone had been dancing around Martha's storyline because her experience suddenly made it political. But taking this risk was a real opportunity to reach the demographic that did watch a lot of Channel 9: non-Indigenous people aged thirty onwards who probably hadn't interacted with any Aboriginal and Torres Strait Islanders before—especially members of the Stolen Generation. It was because everyone took Leah's advice that fans of the show began to gain greater understanding of the impact of past policies and could appreciate the emotional trauma that ripples down the generations. 'Stolen generations', 'unwed mothers'—any art that illustrates the very human stories behind the words helps create empathy, understanding and, I hope, helps to bridge the gap between Indigenous and White Australia.

For a really long time, I thought it was enough to just focus on being a good actor. I never thought of myself as a writer. I didn't think I had anything particularly interesting to say, let alone the ability to convey something through film. Working with people like Leah Purcell and Wayne Blair and watching the art of people like Nakkiah Lui changed my idea of myself and what I can do.

So, even though Josh and I met at a time when I was doing well in my career, he brought me an opportunity that meant I would add another string to my bow and more skills to enable me to stay involved in an industry that I was so passionate about working in.

I had been working quite consistently as an actor, but as persistent as I was with chasing this career, it was my only trade. I remembered the last time it was quiet on the work front. I didn't want to go back to Maccas.

I put that same tenacity and focus I had always had for acting into making *Top End Wedding*. You can have the best ideas, a brilliant script, incredible talent and a vision that blows everyone away but if you don't have the money it is all for nothing. What all films really need is financial support. Movies get more and more costly the further away they are from Sydney, Melbourne and the Gold Coast. And most of the places Josh and I hoped to set the film were in the middle of nowhere. To get people and equipment to these isolated areas was going to be expensive for a production company. We did our research and decided our best bet for financial backing to make the trailer was through Tourism NT.

We thought they would be thrilled to finally have a film set in the Top End without a murder, a crocodile or a murderous crocodile. One that celebrated all that is great about the place—but we also needed to make sure they knew it wasn't a 90-minute ad. It was a ground-breaking rom-com.

Excecutive producer Glen Condie set up a meeting with Tourism NT to discuss our idea. When Josh introduced me to the executive general manager as an actor, he asked, 'What have you been in?'

Josh then told him I was in *Love Child* and *The Sapphires* and the man shrugged and said, in what I thought was the sign of a true businessman's disinterest, 'Oh, those mustn't be in my demographic.'

I hadn't expected this person to know my work—and I think everyone can relate when I say I don't get around to watching all the films and television shows—but I watch stuff that isn't in my demographic all the time. In that moment I interpreted his words as a cold dismissal, and I began to think he really didn't want to give us the money.

Turned out he loved the idea of the film being a love letter to the Territory, and with his support Tourism NT funded the trailer and would go on to fund a significant amount of the film. We were away!

The truth was, we didn't have *that* much money, so we still had to call in favours. We paid Josh's friends to help out—a director of photography affectionately called Fraggle and a sound recordist known by his last name, Rex, came on board. We all crashed at my parents' place because there was no money for accommodation.

We shot most of the trailer at Buley Rockhole, a natural swimming hole in Litchfield National Park. It's roughly two hours' drive from Darwin, and it's basically where everyone hangs out on long weekends. A very healing place, its cascading rapids make all the rockpools feel like natural spas. Its crystal blue water and red rocks surrounded by pandanus and palm trees make you realise you're in an oasis. I highly recommend you look it up on Tripadvisor.

We had already done some filming when we headed there but our time in paradise was short-lived. We were walking into the park when Rex started to feel dizzy. He told us that he was seeing double. Before we got there he had spoken about finishing a first-aid course and they had spent a lot of the time learning how to treat snake bites, and now he was adamant that he had been bitten by a snake.

I was torn about what to do because we had been walking through land that had been cleared off by seasonal burning. We weren't walking through any scrub, so we would have seen a snake before it had bitten Rex. We had all had two coffees on our way there, not drunk a lot of water and had been filming under the hot Australian sun, so I wondered whether Rex might have been just severely dehydrated. But I didn't want to take that chance, so we sent him to hospital. If you're in the bush like that, you should always, always, take things like potential snake bites seriously.

Thankfully, it turned out Rex hadn't been bitten, and he was suffering dehydration. He was terribly embarrassed but we had shot what we needed, and it's better to be safe than dead. I suspect that fearing getting bitten by a snake while walking through snake country after a first-aid course isn't an uncommon reaction.

I was really proud of the trailer, and both Josh and I could see the essence of the film we wanted to make. If we showed producers a pitch trailer and they agreed to make it with us, we'd then get the funding we needed to write the script.

Josh and I wanted this to be more than just a clash of the cultures story. Obviously we didn't have all the answers yet, but we wanted to show the Top End in all its glory. We managed to show the beautiful sweeping landscapes of the Territory, particularly out at Litchfield and Darwin. Thanks to Tourism NT, we also had access to some wonderful stock footage that showed beautiful parts of Kakadu and Katherine. Our trailer managed to capture an idea that was both funny and moving.

We just needed others to feel the same. We showed our trailer to Goalpost Pictures, the production company behind *The Sapphires*. Kylie Du Fresne, one of the producers, said to us, 'I want to know what happens next!' It was an amazing thing to hear. Josh and I needed to be paid while we wrote, and helping the producers visualise the film with that trailer meant that we didn't spend months waiting to hear back about a script that we wrote in our free time. It would have taken us years!

Knowing we had backing made things easier. It gave Josh

and me both the space to commit all our creative energy to this project. Being the more experienced writer, he had the first pass of the script, which meant having the unenviable task of starting with a blank page. He lived in country Victoria while I lived in Sydney. One of the biggest things I learned from him was how to move a story forward. But that means coming to terms with not being able to say everything that you want to say. The thing I really stuggled with was—how do you talk about things like race and interracial marriage with the nuance it deserves in ninety pages? Oh, the joys of screenwriting!

I knew that writing was going to be hard work, but I also felt invigorated and excited to write a story that was so close to my heart. I wanted to show the Territory in a positive light. I wanted to show a loving Aboriginal family, the kind that I grew up in. I wanted to create a rom-com that audiences fell in love with. I was excited by the idea that, one day, people were going to see this on the big screen. And working with Josh, I knew this was going to happen. As far as my career was concerned, everything was going right. But the crazy thing was, just as I was starting to write a romantic comedy my love life was heading totally in the wrong direction. I was definitely the heroine at the start of the feature—single, brokenhearted and deciding to focus on work rather than risk being hurt again.

CHAPTER SEVEN

YOU'VE GOT (A) TWEET

Single people should be commended. It's bloody expensive. If you want to have your own place in a city like Sydney, you have to be raking in some serious coin. Only crazy-rich people go find themselves after a break-up on some *Eat Pray Love* journey. The rest of us have to grind until we own it. Thank you Beyoncé for that beautiful Psalm.

Being in a relationship comes with so many comforts. But it's also the safe choice. Why are so many couples revered when doing something without someone to lean on is a much greater achievement?

Even though I was now living in a dingy little studio apartment, I was only just around the corner from the people who meant the world to me. Most of these girlfriends I would call Cudjeri and my male friends I called Muligah. These terms of endearment helped me feel grounded on Gadigal land, and reminded me that I wasn't alone in that huge, cement forest.

My friends had all helped me move out after my break-up five or six months before. It had been the longest committed relationship I'd ever been in. I was twenty-four when I met this person, and I truly believed I was going to spend the rest of my life with them. I believed no one had noticed me like this person had and the world around me had never felt so bright. Although four mostly happy years went by, we got to the point where we wanted different things from the relationship. I was just beginning to write *Top End Wedding* when we finally went our separate ways.

As heartbroken as I was, a friend had said to me, 'Cudjeri, you didn't move to this city for love, you moved here to follow your dreams.' Even though it was something I knew, it was lovely to hear this from someone else. I made this my mantra and hopped onto my computer and applied to rent the first place in the area I could afford. I had saved up all of my *Love*

Child money to buy a blue Toyota Yaris called 'Belle' (a real cutie), and the rest I used to move into my own apartment.

My dad was down in Sydney for a conference the weekend I moved in, and like any great dad he came over to help me unpack. Sounds great: I get to see my dad and also get help lugging boxes and assembling furniture. It was all going well until ... Unfortunately the stairs of the car park had not been well lit, and rather than abandon the mission he soldiered on but tripped and fell. I was upstairs in the apartment when I heard an unfamiliar-sounding voice calling my name. I had never heard my dad in so much pain. I hurried towards the voice and found him covered in blood. Fear overtook me because I wasn't sure how badly he was injured. I hadn't seen my dad so hurt and vulnerable before. I called an ambulance and they rushed him to St Vincent's Hospital. As soon as he arrived at Emergency they treated him quickly, which is almost always a sign that things might be serious, but after attention and monitoring they released him and we were back at his hotel by midnight. We were both shaken by how quickly calamity had occurred. Dad had a detached retina and a broken hand, but he was alive. A fall like his could have been much, much worse.

It took years for my dad to be paid out the compensation for his injuries, but he recovered fast enough. I'm relieved he had been treated by a doctor for his eye so quickly, otherwise he could have been permanently blinded.

Telling Mum was hard. Initially she was worried, then relieved to find out he would be okay. But there was more bad news for her. My mum had turned sixty that year and had been looking forward to her and Dad going on a Mediterranean cruise. They had never really travelled when I was a kid, there was always something that took priority. The last time they had gone overseas together on a holiday was in 1999, when I was turning twelve.

They were due to fly out three weeks after Dad's fall but the doctor told him after the accident that he was in no condition to fly, let alone fly to Europe. They had to cancel the trip and then they were told they wouldn't receive any refund for the cruise they were booked on. It was a disaster.

Mum was sympathetic to what happened, but she was also annoyed that my dad had even attempted to walk down those stairs in the dark. She understood that the stairs should have been lit, but she also thought that Dad should have been more mindful of what he was doing. It became a prickly topic of discussion, which was made worse when the real estate agency passed the property on to another agency, which made it harder for us to chase up compensation.

It wasn't a great day for any of us and I felt guilty that my dad had been helping me out when he hurt himself. I stayed with him that night and by the time we both got to sleep it was almost morning. I had a 6am start that day for *Love Child*. It was the last day of shooting and when I woke I saw I had several missed calls from production and some of the cast, asking where I was. My stomach dropped. I always made a conscious effort to allow a full hour-and-a-half for my commute even if the distance didn't require it. The traffic out to Western Sydney can be horrendously congested because of the lack of public transport but I preferred to drive so that I didn't have to travel alone at night on the train. Hot in the face, I called the first number back, letting the second assistant director (2AD) know what had happened to my dad. Thankfully, most of the crew knew that something must have been up because it was so out of character for me. I hate being late to work. I know it's not tolerated in many work places, but on sets and stages—time is money. I'm acutely aware that the people behind the scenes can't just stop everything until you get there. A lot of Australian stage and screen productions don't have a huge budget behind them, so they try not to spend that budget on overtime. This means there is a very tight schedule for everyone. In the first few years of being in the industry

I had not managed my time well and had been pulled up on it. In this industry, people have the memories of elephants, so they never forget the time they were inconvenienced by your tardiness.

But being late wasn't just about the cost to me, it was about perception. The last thing I want to do is confirm the stereotype many non-Indigenous people already want to believe about Aboriginal and Torres Strait Islander people— that the majority of the wider community have a poor work ethic and don't know how to rock up on time. Regardless of whether my non-Indigenous co-workers consider this to be true or not, it's a sickening feeling to be reduced to being the actor who doesn't know how to be punctual. Once that mark is against your name, that's all people choose to remember about you. I've also been in professional spaces where an actor who also happens to be Aboriginal is late and my own sense of panic when waiting for the actor to arrive has felt quite heightened. My non-Indigenous peers may think I just hold myself to a higher standard, and I do, but also, I end up in a lot of environments where I'm made to feel as if my failures fall on every Aboriginal and Torres Strait Islander. In my experience in this industry, I feel as if there's a bit more leniency with the non-Indigenous peers, in that personal failure only falls on the individual. So naturally, when I was teased by my fellow actors on *Love Child*, I had a hard time playing along. Especially when that was the first time I'd been late across the whole shoot. Once I had told them what happened to my dad, they were all sympathetic.

Even though it was a rough start to living in my new place, I found self-validation in being independent again. And I had finally made the effort to get my driver's licence. I had procrastinated with getting my licence up in Darwin, and then I couldn't afford a car while I was studying at NIDA, but as *Love Child* was being shot in Parramatta while I lived in Five Dock, where public transport wasn't incredibly convenient to get to, it was time. So, at the tender age of twenty-seven, I was on my Ps and loving driving my friends around.

Of course I drove with a soundtrack! It was around nine o'clock on a Sunday night, and I was driving to my friend's home after dinner in a nice Thai restaurant in the now very hipster Surry Hills. I let my phone play random songs through Bluetooth. My friends love soul, funk, hip-hop and R&B, and though I do too they aren't the songs I love to drive to. If you came across my music favourites on my phone before you saw me, you'd be convinced that I was a platinum-blonde fifty-five-year-old woman named Cheryl.

Normally I tried to hide my true musical self but on this night, with a carload of friends, all of a sudden John Farnham's 'Two Strong Hearts' blasted through the speakers. 'Farnsy' is played at every pub here in Australia, and his most famous song 'You're the Voice' is played in a ridiculous riot montage in Lonely Island's film *Hot Rod*.

'What … *is this*????' shrieked all my passengers in unison. '*Who even are you and why are we friends?*'

It was utter sacrilege to them that Farnsy was playing in their presence. But I couldn't hide it any longer. Belle has a little screen that shows the artist and the track that's playing. It was shared with everyone in the car.

'Shut up and leave me alone!' I yelled back.

Before I knew it I was being called 'Sadie' after the cleaning lady in another of his songs. My mate, Adam Briggs, rapper and music snob, photoshopped my face to an old maid. I wanted the ground to eat me up. My dork factor ramped up big time.

You've quite possibly hurled this book across the room in disgust over my taste in music. I know this music isn't deep, but I grew up with my dad playing Bryan Adams, Bruce Springsteen, Foreigner, Toto, Belinda Carlisle, Fleetwood Mac—basically all the stuff that Smooth FM plays now. My dad had saved up for a fancy stereo to play CDs in the nineties, before discmans came along. My mum also had the soundtracks to *Flashdance* and *Pretty Woman*. I remember being five and playing Roxette's 'It Must Have Been Love' and Go West's 'King of Wishful Thinking' over and over, which got so unbearable for my mum that she gave me headphones so she didn't have to hear the same song on repeat. As I got older I watched films such as *The Bodyguard* and *Dirty Dancing* with my parents—basically films with iconic soundtracks. So, I was my parents' daughter and as far as I am concerned, Smooth FM is not to be sneered at.

What doesn't help the situation is that most rom-coms have these tragic numbers. 'Love is All Around' in *Four Weddings and a Funeral*. 'I Say a Little Prayer' in *My Best Friend's Wedding*. 'Can't Take My Eyes Off of You' in *10 Things I Hate About You*. So, combine my obsession for rom-coms with my musical heritage and it's not surprising I ended up with Farnsy on Belle's playlist and at the receiving end of the scorn of all my friends. I could deal.

At that time, I really did get by with a little help from my friends. They and work (and some great music) saw me through that break-up. I did what I've always done when things haven't worked out in a relationship: I went back to work. It's how I felt validated. The cast of *Love Child* were a lovely bunch to work with, and I looked forward to going in to work every day. I would often give cheek to my mate Andy Ryan—who played Martha's husband Doctor Simon Bowditch—especially when it came to the State of Origin. We had a bet going. Whoever's team lost had to wear the guernsey of the winners. Sadly that year, Queensland won. So I had to wear maroon. I am still mad about it.

As I built my career, people around me began to see that there was more to me than meets the eye—and it was nice to be given the chance to bring my perspective to characters that weren't originally written as Aboriginal. I had experience to show for it. Across this time I made guest appearances in *Secret City*, *Wolf Creek* and *Cleverman*. After the break-up, busying myself with all these wonderful opportunities reminded me what I was capable of. Obviously any break-up can make you lose a bit of confidence in yourself, and while it's not always healthy to attach all of your worth to work, it helps to remember the things you're great at.

The good thing about being an only child is that you get used to your own company, so while I loved my mates, I wasn't needy or desperate for companionship. But I was single.

I know I'm not alone when I say that the dating world can be incredibly blasé. The casual nature of dating wasn't for me, so I decided to stop trying to look for sparks that weren't there. It's probably old-fashioned of me, but until I met my ride or die, I wasn't interested. In the meantime, I refused to be Bridget Jones swigging on vodka and lip syncing to 'All by Myself'.

The only problem was, it's hard to write a film about two people in love when you're trying to believe in love again.

I was writing a film with *wedding* in the title, so it was important to do my research and watch other films that also have *wedding* in the title. However, it's not the healthiest thing to do after you've recently been through a break-up. I made the mistake of watching *My Best Friend's Wedding*, which I hadn't seen since I was a kid with my mum. Boy did this movie creep up on me. In case you haven't watched it—Julia Roberts plays Julianne, a woman who goes to great lengths to stop her best friend Michael (Dermot Mulroney), from marrying Kimmy (Cameron Diaz). After many years of being platonic, Julianne realises she wants to be more than Michael's friend. They've known each other for so long that Tony Bennett's cover of 'The Way You Look Tonight' is their song. There's a scene where it plays and Michael recognises the tune, he takes hold of Julianne and they slow dance to it. When Julianne finds out that the bride- and groom-to-be don't have a song, it further convinces her that she, not Kimmy, is meant to be with Michael. But of course Michael chooses Kimmy over her. Julianne eventually realises that 'the world is just as it should be—for my best friend has won the best woman'. She lends the newlyweds 'The Way You Look Tonight' for their wedding dance 'until you two find your song'. Yes, I did start to sniffle.

Then Michael and Kimmy are sent off by their hundreds of guests. Julianne is trying to run through the crowd to say goodbye to him, but he's nowhere to be seen. She never got to say goodbye to her best friend. Trying her best to hide her disappointment, Julianne starts to head back to the reception. Then someone takes her hand—it's Michael. He hugs his best friend goodbye. He had muscled through the crowd just to find her. By then I was a big snotty mess, sobbing uncontrollably. I started freaking out thinking 'What the hell is happening to me?' because I just couldn't stop bawling. I had finally become Bridget Jones. Damn it. The sacrifices you make for your art.

As much as I wanted to meet someone new, it wasn't happening, so it was actually lovely to live vicariously and create such a wonderful relationship between Lauren and Ned.

For people who haven't seen *Top End Wedding* yet (available on iTunes in Australia *and* North America. No excuse.), Lauren and Ned go on a very hectic chase across the Top

End of Australia in search of her mother, who has clearly had enough and decided to walk out on her dad without notice. Following clues she's left behind—*Hangover* style—Lauren and Ned arrive at a hotel shaped like a crocodile, at which point Ned absolutely loses his mind. Lauren rolls her eyes at him and says, 'Don't look so excited,' and he says to her, 'What do you want from me? I'm walking into a giant crocodile!'

I love this scene because you can see that despite the pressure of having ten days to get married, Lauren and Ned are meant to be together. Josh and I wanted to show a couple who enjoy each other's company and genuinely want to make it work. Lauren has the ability to ground Ned. Ned is good for Lauren because he makes her stop and smell the roses.

A lot of men in rom-coms are jerks, which was one thing I was very keen to avoid. I wanted this film to show a relationship that every person deserves: one of mutual respect. Lauren and Ned didn't have to be married to be happy, but the fact that it was their choice to get married makes it more special.

As *Top End Wedding* was moving along I came to realise that this was the sort of relationship I wanted. But the odds of meeting someone weren't high when I was solely focused on work. I was okay with that.

Then I met James.

One of my best friends Nakkiah (Lui) had asked a writer on Twitter if he was Aboriginal. He tweeted back that he was a European mutt. Being one of the writers on *Gruen* and *The Weekly with Charlie Pickering*, his tweets were very funny and he was joking online with a lot of Aboriginal writers I was friends with. When I looked at his picture, he seemed cute. When I followed him he tweeted, '*Uuuuuh now I'm going to be nervous to ever tweet again. Thank you for freeing me from this website.*'

I was single and he was cute, so I thought: I've got nothing to lose.

[James's note: Miranda has conveniently left out
the fact that she slid into my DMs to apologise for
'missing a show' I was performing in the week before.
We didn't know each other the week before AND the
show was in another city. It was almost as if she had
an ulterior motive.]

Yes, I did have an ulterior motive, because there are so many things I take into consideration before I meet up with someone. Do our political views align? What kind of baggage does he have and is it something I can shoulder? Does he want a long-term relationship? I wanted to know more information before I made such a hasty decision. I don't know if 'slid into my DMs' is an ideal description but, yes, I decided to direct message James so I could find out how we could meet up in person. When I had dinner with Nakkiah I asked her for information on James. I can be very charming when you meet me in person, but for some reason that charm doesn't translate when I text someone I like. Nakkiah had only met James in person briefly when they were on a writing panel together, but like every great friend, she gave me advice, because as everyone knows, texting can be a landmine. I had no idea how to start the convo, so she suggested to bring up his gigs, including a live comedy show he'd hosted a week before.

[James's note: It would be years before I found out that the sweet first texts with my future wife were actually being workshopped by a focus group. Apparently this is much more common than I realised.]

Just as a side note, this isn't a catfish story. Like I said before, James wasn't a total stranger, because he was friends with people I knew. But a girl's still gotta check out what a man's like, right? Most of his photos were of him hanging with very attractive women. I said to Nakkiah, 'What if he's dating one of them?' And Nakkiah rolled her eyes and said, 'Miranda, I know these women—they're lesbians. They're cute but he's not their type.'

[James's note: On the other side, my good friend Bec was sending me intel that apparently Nakkiah had been doing background checks on me because her friend Miranda liked me. It was a nice, if terrifying, surprise.]

I found out James was living and working in Melbourne, so I let him know that I had booked an acting job there. The only problem was, I had already arranged to fly back on the same day. When I told him I couldn't see him, he was all right with that and let me know he would be back in Sydney in a couple of months' time.

When I landed in Melbourne that morning for my day trip, I received a text from James. It was a picture of Melbourne's overcast skyline and a message telling me to keep warm because it was going to be a cold day. I thought it was adorable that he remembered I was going to be in the same city as him.

Then, during the lunch break, I got busted. The women in the production crew caught me smiling at my phone. D'oh! So, I told them about the lovely young man I was speaking to, how he lived in Melbourne and how I was disappointed to have to fly back to Sydney that same day. They were excited on my behalf and told me I was on a flexible flight and it could be changed so I could fly back to Sydney the next day.

This seemed so spontaneous and crazy … I just had to do it.

I didn't want to come across as needy by telling James that I had changed my flights *especially* to see him. Instead I told him we had gone overtime on the ad, that I had missed my flight and was going to fly the next day. I told him I would like to see him if he hadn't any other plans.

[James's note: Look, she sounds really sweet but let's be clear—this whole relationship is built on a lie. Here I was thinking I was providing comfort to a stranded traveller. Gosh.]

Not even, James, you were so keen! There definitely were butterflies fluttering around in my stomach. I told myself of course he would have plans.

[James's note: It's very sweet of her to think this and goes to show how she didn't know me yet.]

Thankfully, James texted me back and told me that he wanted to see me and he suggested we meet at Degraves Street. Yes, it was the most tourist-y place in Melbourne but I didn't know my way around very well and he was sweet enough to pick an easy place for me to get to.

[James's note: I had only just moved to Melbourne and didn't know anywhere. I thought, 'Miranda is fancy and this is the only fancy place I know.' It's not fancy but that shows how little I knew.]

So, I asked hair and make-up to freshen me up, and I went into the city. I was wearing a navy-blue dress, black stockings and ankle boots. I felt cute. I hoped he thought so too.

[James's note: She looked very cute.]

Then he arrived, and my heart nearly burst out of my chest. I thought he was gorgeous. I was so nervous, but I kept it together. We sat at one of the first tables we saw.

[James's note: I've been playing it very cool so far but, reader, you should know that I was terrified. I had only told one work colleague that I was meeting up with Miranda. To this day she recounts having 'never seen anyone sweat so much'. I secretly raced home between work and our date just so I could shower and change my shirt.]

To be fair, I had sprung this date on him at the eleventh hour. I was glad he got back to me so quickly.

Okay—here's a tip to dating an Aboriginal woman: ask her where her mob are from. Like, her people. We are not the Sopranos. It shows that you know that Aboriginal people are not a monolith and you are interested in learning more about who she is.

When James asked me where I was from, I absolutely adored him then and there. I decided he was a lovely nerd the moment he started to talk about space.

[James's note: Space is cool.]

Look, I learned a lot, but I think he noticed my eyes beginning to glaze over because he changed the subject by mentioning that he played the *Django Unchained* soundtrack when he's running or at the gym. This was crazy, because I used the soundtrack for the same thing.

Before we knew it, we were talking about hip-hop and rap, movies we liked and all the things we had in common. It was just so easy to be in his company. There was no judgement between us, and even though we'd only just met, I felt like his equal, that there was some validity in how I saw the world. He wanted to know what I thought.

[James's note: I can still remember the moment she first looked up at me and smiled. I thought, 'Oh no, I'm going to fall in love with her.' Honestly, at that stage it just felt like a big hassle that would definitely hurt a lot in the long run.]

I only knew the guy for, like, a second, but I really, really didn't want us to part. After that night, I knew I wanted to spend more time with James than one day. I looked forward to the moments when I would see him next. I had been cast in a Justin Fleming play called *The Literati* at Griffin Theatre. Directed by Lee Lewis, the play was based on Moliere's *Les Femmes Savantes*. I was lucky to work with some of the funniest actors I've ever met—Kate Mulvaney, Jamie Oxenbould, Caroline Brazier and Gareth Davies. Months passed and I kept going back and forth to Melbourne to spend weekends with James. It worked out really well that he would be working back in Sydney by the time we opened.

A few months after that first date, I was working when I saw many missed calls from friends. I was in rehearsals and normally I don't answer my phone when I am working but I received a follow-up text from Shari to say that it was really important that I call her. I found out that a dear friend of ours, David Page had passed away. He played my uncle in *Yibiyung*, and uncle in Nyoongar language is Konkan. I always called him Konkan after that. Konkan brought so much light into a room, and when he stepped out on stage, he was something to behold. He was also one of the funniest people I knew. I think in taking all the steps to be the best performer I could possibly be, I forgot to have fun. Konkan reminded me that we have to enjoy what we're doing, otherwise why are we doing it? He was a darling of the theatre world and taught me to be fearless, to laugh at my mistakes and to love unconditionally. I was devastated to hear he passed away.

Shari was doing a play called *Bright World* with Guy Simon in Melbourne, and told me to fly down. Lee Lewis, my kind and thoughtful director, hopped in a cab with me to the airport. She asked if I wanted her to stay at the airport with me, and I felt terrible because I could hardly think straight as the reality of grief was settling down and messing with my brain. All I wanted to do was call James.

I'm surprised James could comprehend what I was trying to tell him, because I felt incomprehensible. All James wanted was to be with me and make sure I was okay. Knowing he was waiting for me in Melbourne made me feel better.

I sat on the plane, wrapped in my grief. I had no idea what was happening around me. Konkan worked for Bangarra and, coincidentally, when the snacks trolley came past I was handed a pack that was covered with images of the company's dancers. I don't know if I believe in spirits or angels, but if they do exist, that would have been his way of telling me he was going to be all right. I held onto this packet and sobbed.

I wish my friends Shari and Guy had met James in better circumstances, but despite everyone's grief, that day they brought him into the fold like he was family. James and I went to watch Shari and Guy in their play that night and afterwards we had dinner together in some hipster pub in St Kilda where I played Giant Jenga dreadfully.

[James's note: I still have video of that part.]

Later, I walked along St Kilda beach with James. The passing of my friend made me realise that life is too precious to waste. So, I made him sit on a bench and I told him I loved him. Thankfully, he told me he loved me too.

[James's note: What Miranda didn't know was right as she said it, a crack of lightning hit over the St Kilda pier. Pretty magical. I'm not one to tempt the gods of fate.]

Listen, throw up all you want—we're gross. Yes, our story might be more like *You've Got Mail*, and I'm Joe Fox and James is Kathleen Kelly, but what was so great about co-writing a romantic comedy was that while doing it I realised the kind of man I wanted to connect with. It was important for me to know what I wanted out of a relationship. The process of writing it felt like in *Sleepless in Seattle* where Annie Reed (Meg Ryan) is listening to Sam Baldwin (Tom Hanks) chat about his late wife on talkback radio, saying: 'Well, it was a million tiny little things that, when you added them all up, it just meant we were supposed to be together, and I knew it. I knew it the very first time I touched her. It was like coming home, only to no home I'd ever known. I was just taking her hand to help her out of a car and I knew. It was like … magic.'

Then she spends the rest of the film not quite being able to put her finger on why she was so drawn to this guy, but he was the kind of person she wanted in her life.

So, I think writing a romantic comedy made me think really hard about what I wanted, so that when a man came along whose qualities matched everything I had written about, well, it made sense not to mess around. I hope James can forgive me for this tiny little thing of trapping him, but I'm glad lightning struck.

I'm not perfect and neither is James **[James's note: WHAT!?]**—but the mutual respect and compassion we have for one another will help overcome the things that hold us back.

Months went by and we only got closer.

I found very quickly that if I tell him I don't like something, he'll go ahead and make sure whatever irritates me exists in close proximity. For instance, he began singing 'Islands in the Stream', which I find irritating, but instead of stopping, he just sings it louder. I've bought earplugs.

I don't know what the future holds for us. All I know at this point is that James makes me incredibly happy. He's the person who calms me when I'm feeling overwhelmed and stressed with work. If I project that onto him, he kindly reminds me that he is here to make things easier, not harder. I constantly worry that with my life and my personality he'll want to leave. But he's crazy enough to stay.

I think this is why I love rom-coms so much. Yes, you could argue that many of them are about men getting rewarded for being horrible. One of my favourite moments in *When Harry Met Sally* is when after many hilarious attempts by Harry to get Sally to answer her phone, she finally says to him, 'I can't do this anymore. I am not your consolation prize. Goodbye.'

In *Top End Wedding*, there is no reward for being horrible. The men aren't perfect, but they are good men. I had found that good man for me in real life and now I had to find the right man for our lead character, Lauren.

CHAPTER EIGHT

PAN GYFARFU MIRANDA Â GWILYM

(NO IT'S NOT A TYPO, IT'S WELSH)

THE PRE-PRODUCTION SIDE OF *Top End Wedding* WAS going brilliantly. We had secured actor, award-winning director of *The Sapphires* and proud Batjala Mununjali Wakkawakka man Wayne Blair to direct, and the many jigsaw pieces required to create a film were falling into place. I was learning all the time and was blessed to be working with many talented and generous people who shared the vision of what this film would be. I learned so much about the casting process from filling the roles for *Top End Wedding*. I was playing the lead female role of Lauren, the bride-to-be in the film, and while Wayne was very open-minded with the inputs I gave, I knew he was the captain of the ship. It was important to him and the casting agent, Kirsty McGregor, that there be an ease between me and my co-star. If we could relate to one another, then that empathy would translate onscreen.

The screenplay of a romantic comedy really sings when the two leads have a rapport. It's what glues the story together. It is universally known that the chemistry between Tom Hanks and Meg Ryan is so palpable that for ninety-plus minutes all the audience cares about is if their characters will admit they love each other.

In saying that, life does not need to imitate art in the way it did for *The Notebook* co-stars Ryan Gosling and Rachel McAdams, who fell madly in love off-screen. While their performances were breathtaking and their romance seemed genuine, it wasn't long until it fizzled out. Acting can be mentally and emotionally draining. To be convincing you have to be present. It would have been difficult to dissolve all the feelings that the roles of Ally and Noah would have conjured up—but sadly they couldn't hold on to the magic the film had brought them.

Every actor's process is different, but let's be real—it would have been unsustainable for Bryan Cranston to actually make and sell meth like Walter White in *Breaking Bad*; he'd be in gaol. This is why I'm all for researching and using my imagination. Don't get me wrong, letting all the character's feelings and desires fall away doesn't mean I didn't share something special in that moment with the other actor. But what happens in front of the camera is sacred and, like everything, is only temporary.

Since I was going to play Lauren, Wayne wanted me to read the other lines for the actors auditioning to play her fiancé—or as James so kindly put it, 'Sit in a room and check out hunks.'

Have I told you the script outline yet? Maybe not. So, *Top End Wedding* follows Lauren and Ned, two lawyers in love and living together in Adelaide. Lauren grew up in Darwin with her Tiwi mum and non-Indigenous dad, and she's estranged from her mother's side of the family. As much as Lauren wants to meet them, it has always been a sore spot for her parents.

Ned is uncertain about so many aspects of his life—his career, the unresolved grief over his late father—but one thing he is certain about is his love for Lauren. He can't imagine his life without her. Which is why, after he loses his job, he wants to make her his wife. But in the rom-coms I know and love, having the two lovers make it down the aisle becomes a whole lot more complicated than either of them ever thought it would.

I'm not alone when I say that I'm still intimidated by the audition process. I've got better over the years but I don't think my nerves will ever leave me. I am my own worst enemy, judging myself rather than being in the moment. It wasn't until I began reading as Lauren that I realised an actor's performance can't be judged like an athlete's performance.

Casting is surprisingly subjective. While you might be an excellent performer, it's your essence that gets you the part. It is something I knew even as a young girl when I watched Everlyn Sampi in *Rabbit-Proof Fence*. Everyone brings an aspect of their personality to a role, even Daniel Day-Lewis or Meryl Streep. I'm not saying that those actors are exactly like their characters, but it is their perspective on a role that the director wants. It doesn't hurt to have a name either, which is why it can feel ruthless when you're auditioning to get your big break.

Wayne and the lovely casting agent Kirsty auditioned many talented men from Australia and the United Kingdom. While I would trust Wayne's creative choices, I hoped that the actor who played Ned would understand that Lauren can't divorce herself from the intergenerational baggage that comes with being an Aboriginal woman. That she shouldn't have to assimilate for him to love her. I hoped that the actor Wayne chose wouldn't feel emasculated by Lauren being driven or outspoken but rather would ground her when she is overwhelmed by all the mishaps that occur within the ten-day window they have to get married.

Wayne felt that the character of Ned needed to be the Luke Skywalker of *Top End Wedding*. If you're not a *Star Wars* nerd—Ned needed to be an outsider to the world of the story (ours being the Northern Territory) who asks all the questions to which the audience needed answers. It would open up the story to an overseas audience.

We changed Ned to make him originate from the United Kingdom. While Ned lived in Australia with Lauren, having him come across from somewhere else created a real naïvety to where Lauren is from and her ties to the Tiwi community. Finding the right Ned was key.

But, at that point, I needed a break. I had completely burned out. I didn't need to help find the perfect actor at that moment. I needed to spend time with my perfect boyfriend. After the busy year I had co-writing with Josh as well as all my acting gigs, I needed to do something exciting with my money. James and I felt it was time to see the world, while we didn't have kids and a mortgage to stop us. All our hard work needed to be for something. So, we decided to travel Europe via Japan. I had never been the young Australian backpacker who went on Contiki tours across Europe as soon as they turned eighteen, and I wanted to do it before I got too old and cranky to travel (or something happened to stop me ... sorry Dad!).

So James and I ate and drank our way through Tokyo and Osaka, completely owning our nerdiness and checking out comic-book stores and theme parks. On our way to London we stopped over in Helsinki, where the CBD was twinkling with fairy lights for Christmas; after all the mean school kids talking about Santa not being real—they were damn liars.

We had mates in London, so we decided to make that our base while we travelled across Europe. When I got to London I felt completely weird that England still believes it brought industry and organisation to countries like mine. The narrative of Australia has been determined by non-Indigenous Australians for so long, that it's only in the past decade that Aboriginal and Torres Strait Islander academics have truly been heard. This narrative, that any Indigenous culture became civilised by England, is old and simply not true. Man, I wish I had the hand-clapping emoji on me. Ancestors like mine were completely intuitive to the land they lived on. They knew how to farm the land, because they understood weather patterns, what plants were in season and how animals behaved. Archaeologists given permission to dig on the land of the Mirarr (Mir-ray) people of Kakadu discovered evidence of stone axes developed 20,000 years before any other axes that have been found.

Anyway, I'm speaking about this in very simplistic terms, and so I highly recommend you seek out work by Aboriginal and Torres Strait Islander academics and writers to see their perspective on our history. But the point I'm making is that it can be soul-crushing to walk past a statue of Captain Cook near Buckingham Palace, knowing that his arrival meant the beginning of violence and dispossession towards Australia's First People.

Another thing I came to realise was that our national news constantly reports on England, but there was next to nothing about Australia on their news. England neither knows nor cares about Australian politics or society. It makes me wonder why we continue to maintain ties to this place so many Australians with Anglo-Saxon and Celtic ancestry call the motherland. Maybe it's easier for Australians with British lineage to not acknowledge the history before their ancestors arrived because it means having to own up to and dismantle the system that their forebears built. Equality must worry them because they think that things won't be on their terms anymore. Denying it means that people like myself have to waste their precious time proving that different Aboriginal customs and beliefs are valid.

I was so grateful to Josh that he opened up this opportunity for me to write a story that really celebrated Australia through a different lens. While stories that delve into systemic problems that face Aboriginal and Torres Strait Islanders should continue to be told, what we really wanted for *Top End Wedding* was to show non-Indigenous audiences not only what they were missing out on, but also that our desires and aspirations have a place in the mainstream.

Despite those reservations about the United Kingdom, when I got to London I was completely invigorated by a city that appreciated art, history … and rom-coms.

While visiting a Darwin friend living in Notting Hill, I made James—made being the operative word—get in an obligatory photo with me in front of the famous blue door from the film of the same name. The one that Hugh Grant's flatmate opens while wearing nothing but tighty-whiteys and is met with thousands of paparazzi outside hoping for a shot of Julia Roberts. James groaned but he had no say in the matter.

Even though I was having the time of my life on our holiday, I made the effort to check my emails. Kirsty McGregor, who is an all-round legend, had sent me a message practically begging me to take time in my trip to meet a Welsh actor, Gwilym Lee. He had sent audition tapes over from London, and they felt his spirit resonated within Ned.

LESSON IN PRONOUNCING GWILYM: *Gwil-im*.

At first, I wanted to give a hard no. While I'm fully aware how fortunate it is to be a working actor in Australia and also then to have a film you created in the works, I was exhausted. James and I departed a month before Christmas, and a lot of creatives had been desperate to tie up loose ends before the summer holidays began. It had been quite a hectic period of time before we left and we had both been scrambling towards the finish line. To make matters worse, I had lost my passport in my move to Melbourne. (Did I tell you I moved to Melbourne? James was there, so I needn't say more.) I know, I hear your groans of agony (about the passport, not the moving in with James). Earlier in the year I had been at my wit's end with everything I had accumulated in my tiny apartment in Sydney. Most people can relate to the fact I had begun with the good intention of 'Kondo-ing' the space. The novelty of deciding which crap 'sparked joy' quickly wore off and I ended up just tossing things in either boxes or bins, no longer caring where my stuff ended up; I just needed it on the damn removal truck. The passport definitely ended up in a box, because I found it after I cancelled it. But in all the panic leading up to the trip I had no choice but to pay the hefty fee to get a replacement in the shortest time possible. Relief flooded over me when my new (albeit expensive) passport fell into my grateful little hands. My trip wasn't cancelled after all. The cherry on top was that I knew I would be working when I got back, so I was able to clock off completely and have a proper holiday without the niggling thought that I had no work to come back to.

One of the wonderful things to come out of that crazy pre-holiday time was the offer of the role of Rose in Nakkiah Lui's play *Black is the New White*. Just days before James and I flew out, my agents received an email from the casting director of Sydney Theatre Company. They had reached out to gauge my interest. The only problem was, Goalpost were scheduled to start *Top End Wedding*. We were sorting that all out and I was confident it would all happen, so all James and I wanted when we got on the plane was time and space away from work. I wanted to eat cheese and drink wine, see plays with James and catch up with friends. Reading lines for the movie was not what I wanted to do. I needed the break.

A life lesson I've never quite managed to grasp (other than remembering important things like a passport) is the fact that good or bad, circumstances always change. I gave myself a good talking to because I hadn't seen any of Gwilym's work, despite him being on *Midsomer Murders*. I didn't know if he had played a romantic lead in a film before and I hadn't been able to watch the rest of the shows in which he'd acted. Now that I was on his side of the world, it was my opportunity to see if we were going to bond.

Despite knowing this was good for the film I still grumbled my way out of bed and into the shower that morning, and in that time the beautiful man who would become my husband had looked up what platform I was to be on, where to change trains and how far ET casting was from Shepherd's Bush Tube station. He's a bit of all right, my James.

As I was travelling on the Tube I said to myself, 'This is going to be the biggest waste of my time. This Gwilym bloke might be an incredible actor but he's not going to know or care about Australia and we're going to have absolutely nothing in common.'

I met Emily Tilelli the casting agent, who was from Australia. I felt better knowing that people who got where I was from and what the film was about were involved.

I excused myself to the bathroom, and as I was putting make-up on in the mirror it suddenly dawned on me that, after three years, our little film was getting made. Wayne trying to find our Ned meant it was truly coming to life. I felt electrified with joy.

Then I heard a gentle voice come from the waiting room. I could hear happy greetings from the casting ladies. I took a deep breath and packed up my things.

As I stepped out, a good-looking mousy-brown-haired man was sitting in the chair by the doorway.

'Hello, I'm Gwilym,' he said.

Despite probably being (understandably) a bit nervous before his audition, Gwilym was an absolute delight. I was touched by how much he loved the script, that he said it was something he had never read before. I suddenly felt terrible that I had made all these pre-conceived judgements before actually meeting the man, and all of a sudden I caught myself babbling—because that's what I do when I suddenly start caring about what people think of me. I wanted Gwilym to like me.

Even though I struggled to describe the Northern Territory to him, we were able to talk about all the cool places to see and things to do in London. Since it was leading up to Christmas I told him about how we celebrate Christmas in our summer.

I told him about the barbecues and swimming I do on Christmas Day, drinking champagne and eating prawns, and he was genuinely curious. Unlike me, he wanted to hear about my life before he passed judgement.

I tried to downplay how excited I was about seeing snow. I didn't tell Gwilym this, but while James and I had been in London, we danced in snow. There was *snow*! I legitimately felt like Bridget Jones when she runs after Mark Darcy. I may have proclaimed that very loudly in the street when James and I ran out to dance in it.

You don't understand—the most heartbreaking thing I was told when I was five wasn't about Santa, but that it wasn't going to snow for Christmas in Jabiru. My mum had showed me on a map where we were in Australia, and where Santa lived at the North Pole and said the snow didn't travel all the way down to us. It had confused the hell out of me because she had given me all these bloody books about Christmas set in the northern hemisphere! Yes, I'm still devastated, and no, I don't want to talk about it anymore.

The first time I saw snow was when I was in New York for the premiere of *The Sapphires*. I remember this African-American woman who stopped to watched me, clearly concerned for my mental wellbeing.

'It's *snowing*!' I said to her.

'Yeah gurl, it snows every year,' she replied, rolling her eyes.

But nothing could spoil it for me. As you can tell, it still is a massive novelty, seeing as instead of snow at Christmas we get crappy white spray-paint on shop windows and plastic pine trees.

Gwilym told me that he was working on a film, which I would later find out was the Queen biopic *Bohemian Rhapsody*. He was playing Brian May. I'm not sure whether he wasn't allowed to tell me or if he was being terribly British downplaying how awesome that was. He was looking down at his feet so I decided not to press him.

I told him I had Googled him and then apologised for Googling him, because it always comes across as stalker-y to the person you're looking up. He smiled and told me it was okay because he had Googled me as well. I was really glad that we both ended up doing a bit of homework. Then, after all the polite small-talk, we went through the lines.

We went in to the audition and I'll never forget the twinkle in his eye. I had just met the man but already I was making him laugh. I found myself breaking out of character when I noticed how naturally Ned's lines came to Gwilym. He had all the qualities that I envisioned Ned would have: a kind, patient, charming, funny man who was always up for an adventure. He made Ned an optimist, unruffled by the inconveniences that came along for him and Lauren. I got the sense he would easily dismantle any stress or tension with humour. Hwyl, as the Welsh would call it, where someone is full of ardour. Gwil had hwyl.

He barely knew me, but Gwilym seemed to be enjoying my company as much as I was his.

'Well, we seem to have everything,' said the casting agent. 'Is there anything else you'd like to try?'

'No,' said Gwilym, 'unless there was something else you can think of?' he added, turning to me.

'Yeah nah, I thought you were excellent!' I blurted.

'Yay! There you go—positive reinforcement from one of the writers!' said the casting agent. Then she asked him, 'Can you see yourself in the Northern Territory with Miranda?'

'After today?' replied Gwilym grinning at me. 'Absolutely.'

About a day later, the producer, Rose, told me that they were going to offer Gwilym the role. He had apparently asked for the contract the minute he saw the photos of Katherine Gorge and Kakadu. So, that was it. We had our Ned.

That was when Miranda met Gwilym.

CHAPTER NINE

THE PROPOSAL ...
NOT THE SANDRA BULLOCK FILM VERSION

I MIGHT HAVE BEEN A ROM-COM NERD AND ABOUT TO make a film with *wedding* in the title, but the truth is I never thought I would get married. It wasn't because I didn't want to—I did—but like many of my generation, most of the men I dated believed that people who loved one another didn't need to be married to be happy and committed to one another. Or at least that's what they said.

I knew I would be more than enough if I wasn't someone's wife, but—and I blame the brainwashing by all the princess films I grew up with—I have always thought there would be something special about the person I loved becoming my husband. I am embarrassingly hetero.

Growing up watching a happily married couple like my parents just normalised things for me. I wanted to be in a marriage like theirs someday. A lot of people ask how my parents met. This makes my mum feel uncomfortable because she feels her relationship with my dad suddenly gets put under the microscope. Despite people's genuine curiosity, no one else in my parents' social circle gets asked that question. The people who want to know have married someone of the same heritage. I don't think people realise how much their bias manifests in the way they see marriage, let alone in the questions they ask. They ask because they're surprised to see my White dad with an Aboriginal woman. Well, how they met is for them to tell, not me.

What I love about my parents' marriage is that they've never questioned each other's lived experience. The main issue they have in their relationship is my dad leaving his dirty cereal bowl in the kitchen sink. It riles my mum and, in fairness to her, the ants in the Northern Territory get to food much quicker than any insect in the southern states.

Mum and Dad were married in 1976 where, only fifteen years before, it wasn't legal for an Aboriginal woman to marry a non-Aboriginal man without the permission of the Protector of Aborigines. Let me paint a picture of the cultural melting pot Darwin has been and continues to be. Founded in 1869, the city we now know as Darwin is a stone's throw from Indonesia and Timor. Well before the English made their way up from Sydney Cove, Macassans from Indonesia had been trading trepang (sea slug) with Aboriginal tribes across the Northern Territory and north-western Australia since the early 1700s. The Pine Creek gold rush in the 1870s brought many families across from China. The Greco–Turkish war in the 1920s brought many Greek families to Darwin.

Despite how normal it was for me to live among many South-East Asian, Chinese and Greek families, the Australian Government appeared to be terrified of these groups multiplying and thriving. The *Immigration Restriction Act 1901* (which formed the basis of The White Australia Policy) favoured the immigration of Anglo-Saxon people; everyone else was considered 'alien'. The current mandatory-detention policy that stands in Australia should not shock you considering our recent history.

While many Australians are aware of the policies enacted to 'breed out' Aboriginal people, not many know about the policies created to segregate Aboriginal people from the rest of society. It was not as clear-cut as in the United States; indeed as time went on the Australian Government employed more subliminal language so it didn't come across as blatantly racist.

The *Aboriginal Ordinance 1918* was changed to the *Welfare Ordinance 1953–1960*. The amended Ordinance may not have made reference to Aboriginality, but people became wards of the state if they didn't have the right to vote. At this point in time, no Aboriginal person was allowed to vote, which meant they were automatically a ward of the state. How you were deemed a ward of the state was extremely loose, and the goalposts constantly shifted to suit bureaucracy. There were many ways to fall under the criteria of the Ordinance. Basically, if an Aboriginal person sneezed—*Boom!*—ward of the state. It was all about control.

Once a ward, a male was prohibited from being in the company of a female ward between sunset and sunrise, nor could he have sexual intercourse with or live with a woman. A woman was prohibited from the same, nor could she marry without the permission of a Government 'protector' or, in the Northern Territory, have a sexual relationship outside of marriage. The punishment could be a fine or imprisonment, or both.

Way to kill the romance, am I right? God forbid an Aboriginal woman falling pregnant to an Indonesian, Chinese or Greek husband—that would mean some form of colour would continue. The Government having dominance over who an Aboriginal woman married ultimately ensured approval of whom she had children with.

Before 1961, when the federal Government passed the *Marriage Act 1961*, each State and Territory managed their own marriage laws. Even though this was fractured, the laws for marriage for Aboriginal people were similar.

Knowing that if my parents were born a few years earlier their marriage would have been illegal shocked me. It also made me sympathise with Australia's LGBTQI community, who have only very recently been given the right to marry. I completely understand if the LGBTQI mob are sick of talking about marriage; they spent months on end pouring their hearts out only to have many in power ignore their pain. It is galling that it was only in 2004 that then Prime Minister John Howard cemented the definition of marriage as 'voluntarily entered-into union of a man and a woman to exclusion of all others'. From that moment on, no one from the LGBTQI community could legally marry in Australia, and if they eloped overseas their marriage wasn't recognised back in Australia. Mr Howard was reported as saying: 'We've decided to insert this into the Marriage Act to make it very plain that it is our view of a marriage and to also make it very plain that the definition of a marriage is something that should rest in the hands ultimately of the parliament of the nation.'

I think everyone should butt out of everyone else's business, and no piece of paper should stop two loving adults from forming a legal union if that is what they wish. My wonderfully brave and resilient friend Sally Rugg was the marriage-equality campaign director of GetUp at the time of the same-sex marriage plebiscite. Obviously this affected her and the LGBTQI community deeply, and she summed up the fiasco well: 'I'm also a queer woman, and I honestly don't know how it will feel to hold a piece of paper in my hands knowing it might have the power to define my worthiness under the law.'

Learning this history of exclusion and control made me want to get married. I'm living in a time where I have the right to choose. I don't need to be protected from myself. I'm not a threat. I'm not a problem. I didn't have to get married, but if I was in a loving and respectful relationship, my kind partner could propose without getting arrested.

But I had no idea my kind partner was planning just that.

We had only just gotten over our jetlag after our trip from Europe. We had arrived back two weeks away from Christmas. Our mothers would have killed us if we stayed over there for

Christmas Day. It was almost midnight when we got back to our sharehouse in Brunswick and our taxi driver had spent twenty minutes lecturing James to 'treat her right'. Normally I'd enjoy the sentiment, but after a twenty-two hour flight back via Japan (where we had stopped on the way over), I was exhausted.

James and I only had a couple of days to reset our body clocks to the Southern Hemisphere before we took my car, Belle, on a roadtrip along the Hume Highway to Sydney.

The day James wanted to propose, we were all in Sydney and I had booked for us to take my parents to see a matinee performance of a Belvoir St Theatre play. God only knows why my parents leave it to me to organise these kinds of things, because I am the least organised person in the world when it's not about work.

Mum and Dad were down from Darwin for the Christmas holidays and the matinee started at 2pm. The plan was to get there early enough to have a leisurely brunch at a cafe near the theatre. I hate wolfing down food when I haven't given myself enough time to eat it. Also, cafes get busy on weekends! Who knows how long these hipsters will take to serve you?

James had woken that morning to say he needed to pop up to the local shops. It was around 8.30, which was strange for him when we were on holiday—usually he'd still be lying in bed, on his phone. So, I was under the impression he was just getting coffee for Dad, who often went up to get himself one. So, I shamelessly asked James if he could get me one while he was there. There was a confused look on his face before he said, 'Sure.' I asked him if something was wrong, and he assured me there wasn't, gave me a kiss on the forehead and left.

[James's note: So, I had called Miranda's parents a short time earlier and asked for permission to propose. Moments before this, I had ducked out to tell Miranda's father that today was the day and that I was just ducking up to the shops to get a couple of supplies and some champagne. 'I'll tell her I'm grabbing a coffee.' Now I actually had to do a coffee run, too!]

Originally Mum and Dad were travelling to the cafe in Surry Hills in a separate car. Now all of a sudden they insisted on coming with us. I had so much crap in the back seat of Belle that I had to move everything out so they could fit. I was so embarrassed to do this in front of them, because they are incredibly neat and clean. Taking all my stuff out made us twenty minutes behind our schedule.

[James's note: Now, this wasn't part of the plan. This was a miscommunication. For the luckiest day of my life, this was not my lucky day. Miranda was flustered and a little annoyed with me. Off to a great start!]

We headed off, with James driving. But he took the wrong turn to the city and I started to stress out. The last time he veered off to go on an adventure, we got incredibly lost. He wanted to take me on a date to where he grew up—out at Wisemans Ferry along the Hawkesbury River. He had absolutely no idea where he was going because he hadn't been there since he was seventeen, and neither of us had phone reception. We managed to end up at the back of someone's paddock, where a massive bull was roaming free. This bull's eyes locked onto my Belle. He took a step towards us as we drove past him and I may have peed a little. It didn't help that we drove past two old bearded men in a ute on the side of the road and James said, 'Boy, I hope these guys don't Wolf Creek us.' It was then that I began to yell at him: 'That is *not* funny, James! That is very much a reality for a woman from the Territory!' Thankfully, we managed to get back onto the highway to Sydney. Since that date, I have had very little faith in James's sense of time and direction when we are on holidays.

[James's note: Okay. Yup. Gotta take the loss on that one.]

We were going to be late, and James wasn't worried at all. He was playing all these songs from our favourite playlist— 'Bonnie and Clyde 03' by Jay-Z and Beyoncé and 'Marry You' by Bruno Mars. I knew that Mum hated that kind of music, so I turned it down. But Mum just giggled and said, 'It's all right, James, you can play whatever you want.' I couldn't believe this. My mother forever complained about the music I played in the car. Not only did she find my generation's music unnecessarily noisy, she didn't believe I had the ability to concentrate. 'Yes, but James is a better driver,' she said smugly. So now I was being ganged up on in the car.

[James's note: I could see Barbara smiling through the rear-view mirror but I couldn't say anything! Also, to Miranda's credit, I *was* a little lost.]

Then James pulled up outside a park I used to play in as a kid when I came down to Sydney in the school holidays. This park has a lookout and is surrounded by stunning gum trees and the Georges River. It is a beautiful spot ... but not where we were meant to be. Why couldn't we just stick to the day I had planned for us? There was nowhere to eat; nowhere decent, anyway. But James insisted we take a walk up the hill. I was in heels and was not impressed. Then Mum and Dad announced that they had forgotten something in the car so we had to go back to get it.

[James's note: Okay, now Miranda was properly pissed at me and only just holding it in. I was starting to game plan in my head how I would retreat and try this again another day if she finally snapped. Also, I was about to ask the woman of my dreams to marry me, so there was an awful lot to be nervous about.]

Then James hugged me and whispered, 'Isn't this beautiful?' Now it was getting strange. He never thought the Sutherland Shire was beautiful. He was always giving it flack. Why on earth did he want to have brunch *here*? Despite the fact he'd been up to the shops, he hadn't bought any food for a picnic. Then he said to me: 'You make me so incredibly happy, Miranda Tapsell … I can't remember what my life was before I met you.' Then he pulled out a jewellery box. He couldn't even get out, 'Would you do me the honour of being my wife?' before I screamed and hugged him. I started crying and saying, 'I'm sorry, I am such a bitch!' And then he said, 'Wait, are you saying no?' And I said, 'No, I'm saying yes! Yes, I will marry you!'

[James's note: Phew!]

I turned to see my overjoyed parents, who had popped the champagne James bought that morning. We took that bottle to a local cafe overlooking the water. On any other day, I would have found the food abysmal, but that day it was the best food I had ever eaten. It was more than James wanting to make me his wife. It was more than all the fanfare that can come with a wedding. Out of all the people in the world he could have chosen to spend the rest of his days with, he chose me. Even when I'm shrivelled up like Benjamin Button (because that's what I'll look like, a very old child) he signed up for this. Everything that James had done to make me laugh, give me comfort and see things in a new light had brought me a joy and contentment I hadn't known before. All he has ever wanted to do is make me happy. And it's why I can't imagine life without him.

CHAPTER TEN

RESPECTING 65,000 YEARS

BECAME A BRIDE-TO-BE OFFSCREEN MERE WEEKS
before I was about to be a bride onscreen. Honestly,
who does this to themselves? I bet every person who has
ever attended a wedding must be thinking 'Girl, what is the
matter with you?'. I was hopelessly in love and I was about
to shoot a romantic comedy. You would think I wouldn't
have anything to worry about, right? Well, I was frightened.
I knew how I wanted to tell *Top End Wedding* but I wanted
to tell it right.

It comforted me to know that I wasn't the first Aboriginal woman to make the film she wanted to see on screen. Brilliant filmmakers such as Madeline McGrady, Tracey Moffatt and Lorraine Mafi-Williams blazed the trail for not only using film for activism but speaking through the Aboriginal female gaze. Directors Rachel Perkins, Darlene Johnson and Leah Purcell have echoed this and gone on to make the stories they wanted to see on screen. These women are the reason I could make the funny and joyous film I had hoped to make.

I wasn't the first and am certainly not going to be the last. However, we could never be truthful or authentic about the story we wanted to tell if Traditional Owners in Kakadu, Katherine and Tiwi didn't have some input into how we reflected people and country.

This isn't about being politically correct, it was about being thoughtful and having manners. To say hello and fill people in on who you are and what you plan to do on country isn't a massive ask from the Mirarr, Jawoyn and Tiwi people whose land we were filming on. Also, their insight was the very thing that enriched the story.

Many people put their own blood, sweat and tears into this but, as I mentioned many times to Wayne, Josh and the producers, if we just rocked up to either Kakadu, Katherine or Wurrumiyanga with crew and equipment not having spoken to any of the Traditional Owners, it would fall on me, the woman who knew these places and communities to speak to them. I travelled up to these places multiple times with either Josh, Wayne or Rose to meet with Traditional Owners to inform them about what we hoped to do and ask them to help us make that happen.

I didn't want to offend any Traditional Owners or overlook acknowledging connections to any mob in the way it was reported that Don Shirley's family felt they were disrespected during the making of *Green Book*. They say write what you know, but even if I was eighty per cent sure on how we were portraying country and community, I wouldn't have the audacity to assume that the other twenty per cent wouldn't involve conversations with family and Traditional Owners. Even though people flocked to *Once Upon a Time in Hollywood*, Bruce Lee's daughter, Shannon, found that her father was written like a caricature. A lot of people said that could have been avoided had his family been consulted. Having this kind of criticism overshadow what we were trying to achieve in *Top End Wedding* was one of my biggest fears. I like to think I would have the grace to accept when I have fallen short on a project I have attached myself to—but initially it would feel like a punch in the guts because I hurt the people I care about.

Josh had mentioned to Goalpost that he was writing about a place he had never been to. As much as I was happy to share what I knew about Tiwi with him, he needed to get what I was putting in the script. We had managed to find a time that suited us both to go over to the Island. I had gone up to the Territory a couple of times just to make sure everyone, absolutely everyone, knew we weren't going to make it without their blessing. Turns out, that paid off. Both the Gundjeihmi and Jawoyn Association Aboriginal Corporations had given their full support, and now everyone was buzzing with excitement that a film crew was coming to their town. It had been too long since I'd seen my Aunty Yvonne Margurula in Kakadu. She is one of the Traditional Owners and one of the major advocates against the Jabiluka mine development in the late 90s. I would have been dragged by her if the producer, Kate Croser, hadn't driven me out there. One of the blessings of making these connections was putting together my family tree. I wouldn't have done this without the help of Sister Anne Gardiner, a nun who has been on Tiwi for 60 years. She is an integral part of the community. It has always been important to her that Tiwi mob maintain their culture and knowledge of their respective family trees. Sadly, because many of the older members of the community have died, Sister Anne held onto records of family trees, so people could keep track of who their relatives were. I was thrilled to be able to talk about my extended family and how I was related. While we would often see Tiwi family in passing when they caught the ferry to Darwin, living in Kakadu meant we had allowed time to slip away from us and lost touch. I don't really know why Nana Lucy hadn't made the time to go over.

I will always love my Nana Lucy dearly, but she was never one to talk about her feelings or her past. I feel that many women, particularly Aboriginal women of her generation, survived by looking forward. The vibe I got from Nana Lucy whenever I asked questions was that it was a privilege to contextualise your life and what had influenced it up to the present. I don't know if she was given much of a chance to question her place in the world. Like Dory, she just had to keep on swimming. If you wanted to hear a yarn from her, you just had to sit down with her and wait until she was ready to talk about it. Forget about trying to do that between the hours of noon and 2pm on a weekday; this time was booked out for *Days of Our Lives*, *The Young and the Restless* and, a bit later in the day, *The Bold and the Beautiful*. Then Sunday was Church.

Thankfully, my mum has an incredible memory for names and faces, and she shared with me some of our family stories. I was about twenty when I first went over to Wurrumiyanga, and I have never been so excited. I was on term break at NIDA, and catching the ferry over for the day was just the thing I needed. It was a beautiful sunny day sailing over aqua-blue water. The last ferry returning to Darwin would leave in two hours, which meant we didn't have a long time over there. Thankfully Mum knew enough people for us to be driven around Wurramiyanga. With the help of my Mum (and later Sister Anne Gardiner), I would start to piece together the rest of my family tree. Stanislaus Puruntatameri married Cecilia Palamtipaiu and had nine children—Daniel, Alfie, Eugenio, Janie, Tessi, Mary-Anne, Grace, Immaculata and Enid. We visited Tiwi Art where two of my Muningawus (grandmothers) Tessi and Immaculata worked. Tessi and Immaculata made beautiful paintings and carvings there.

I remember when Mum introduced me to one of Nana Lucy's sisters, Enid, and Enid said to me, 'You call me Nana.' She pinched my cheek and slapped it, which surprised me but made me laugh. Not only did I feel loved the minute I arrived, I now knew where my mother had got her incredible memory. All of my Muningawus knew where I sat on the family tree.

They knew who all of their Larrakia family from the mainland were. A lot of Tiwi men told me that they knew my dad from all the travels he made over there.

One of my favourite stories is how some of them believed my mother fell pregnant with me. There is a crystal blue waterhole about a fifty-minute drive outside of Darwin, on the other side of the harbour. It flows at the back of an Aboriginal community called Belyuen, where my parents used to live and work. This is how interconnected Aboriginal people are up in the Top End, they know about everyone else's country, especially when so many Tiwi worked over in Darwin. A lot of Tiwi mob know about this waterhole and know that the local mob living in Belyuen believe it to be a place where women fell pregnant if they swam in it, which my mother had.

'That's how your mother fell pregnant with you,' a few mob told me.

My mum and dad blush when this story is told, but I think the idea of the water making my mum pregnant, especially when becoming pregnant had been such an ordeal is incredibly cute.

Another window I had into Tiwi life was through my Uncle Jason, who is also known as Foxxy Empire. He had written a play called *Wulamanayuwi and the Seven Pamanui*. When

Uncle Jason found out there wasn't a Tiwi version of *Snow White and the Seven Dwarfs* he was inspired to write it.

My friend Shari Sebbens and I were part of the development of the play, we read it at the Darwin Festival and we took it over to the Tiwi Islands as well, performing it at Wurrumiyanga and Milikapiti.

Shari played the Snow White character called Wulamanayuwi and I was playing Jirrakalala, the evil queen. I had so much fun being evil and funny. Uncle knew how to make it very joyous, fabulous and cheeky.

Unfortunately, due to a scheduling conflict I couldn't perform in the play when Belvoir picked it up. But the wonderful thing was that it was such a window into the world of Tiwi; it was lovely to know more about the mob I hadn't grown up with. It was also great to learn Tiwi words with my Aunty Nina Puruntatameri, who was brought on to help us pronounce the Tiwi words properly.

There is a local women's choir on Wurrumiyanga called Ngarakuruwala (We Sing Songs). The singers in the choir are a delegation who call themselves the Wangatunga Strong Women. They are mostly women in their forties to sixties. Dr Genevieve Campbell, a professional French horn player and ethnomusicologist, worked tirelessly alongside the Wangatunga

Strong Women to repatriate archive recordings to document and preserve songs that had been sung in old Tiwi. Genevieve runs the group and they sing in 'Old Tiwi', the more formalised version of the language. 'New Tiwi' is more of a mixture of English and Old Tiwi and is considered slang. Many of the older mob are worried that the old way of speaking will go, but maintaining story and language through song gives me hope. Hearing them sing felt like a gap inside me had filled up.

It can be really hard to get over to the Tiwi Islands in the wet season, which falls across Australian summer and throws out relentless humidity. I thought about taking James over to Wurrumiyanga when I was cruel enough to bring him up for Christmas, but my mother warned against it, telling us that we would most definitely get stuck over there because of all of the monsoonal storms that had been lingering about. Cyclones were forming and travel should be avoided. A few years in Sydney and Melbourne and I'd forgotten about that.

There's only a small window to visit people in the dry season. The weather is more temperate and it's such a great time to go camping that everyone leaves town. As soon as the school holidays are on, everyone shuts up shop. I'm not trying to make up excuses for not going over more often, I bring this up because it was some of the knowledge I needed to draw on to make *Top End Wedding* with the respect the Tiwi community deserved.

Even though I hadn't grown up with my mob on Tiwi, I understood they were on a completely different schedule to the rest of the country. Once you hit their shores you are on their time. I remember having to tell the people at Goalpost that not only did we have to avoid shooting in the wet season, we had roughly a four-month gap before the big term break that went for four weeks. On top of that, the community deserved time to absorb what we were about to do. They needed to be assured our film would celebrate the people and what goes right in the community.

I remember waking up in a cold sweat after having dreamed about my Muningawus, my Aunties, my uncles and the rest of the mob being incredibly hurt and frustrated with how the film was being handled and them saying to me, 'Well, you're family. How could you not know how this would upset us? If you were at the helm of it, why wouldn't you speak up?'

I know it was just a dream, but their opinions mattered to me. That dream made me realise I needed to engage with the community more to know what their boundaries were and also to earn their trust and support. They deserved a seat at the table. I reached out to Libby Collins, who is the community engagement officer at Bangarra Dance Theatre, one of Australia's premier dance companies but also led by an Aboriginal man Stephen Page, with all Aboriginal and Torres Strait Islander dancers. I respect Libby and admire her direct nature and her ability to be as cool as a cucumber under pressure. I feel like maybe Tiwi has taught her how to do that. I shared the script of *Top End Wedding* with her and told her that obviously I wanted this film to be not just about family, but about culture and community. There's plenty of that in Darwin, but as there are still people alive to speak and sing in Tiwi, I wanted to preserve that in film.

Thankfully, Libby told me how much she loved the story. The sick feeling in the pit of my stomach left me. I wanted to build that trust with her, and I wanted her to know that my intentions towards and within the community were good. I also hoped she would pull me up if I did take a wrong step. Libby was going to be more than a consultant on the film, her knowledge was key to making things work. She would be integral to the shoot on the Tiwi Islands. Being a Tiwi woman, she could let the locals know exactly what we were doing on country and why. On top of everything else, she would also be 'wrangling' all the extras we would need on the Island. Essentially, Libby would be the bridge between the crew and the community. I was grateful she could see that I was using the film to reconnect with mob. Her cousin Grace Young, who coincidentally had married into my family, had also helped drive Josh and I around Wurramiyanga and meet with different members of the community.

It wasn't something that was at the forefront of my mind when my co-writer, Josh Tyler, said he wanted to write a rom-com with me, set in the Territory. It was audacious and nerve-wracking to not only write something that had never been written before but to take this idea around to producers, funding bodies and distributors, but my career was built on being thrown in the deep end. So, much of the time, I went with my gut. I really listened to that sick feeling in the pit of my stomach and acted accordingly.

Before Libby and Wayne came on board and we were shopping the idea of the film, I wasn't comfortable being the only Aboriginal creative attached to the project. I was also not comfortable with the assumption that many people had that because I had connections with so many Aboriginal groups in the Top End, I could write honestly and authentically about it all. I may be empathetic and well read, but the wider Aboriginal community has so many facets to it. For instance, the life I have lived as a coastal woman in Darwin is completely different from the one Warwick Thornton has lived as a desert man in Alice Springs.

Even though I had blood relatives on Wurrumiyanga, I didn't grow up in that community—so, when Josh came up with the idea of the bride- and groom-to-be going on this *Hangover*-style road trip, I wanted to take the opportunity to show that regardless of how spread out they are, the Larrakia, Jawoyn, Mirarr and Tiwi communities are incredibly interconnected.

I was born on the Larrakia land of Darwin, my great-grandmother's country.

I grew up with Mirarr mob in Kakadu and I have family there.

I went to Nitmiluk National Park for school camp.

My great-grandmother's husband was from Bathurst Island, and I would visit family with my mum on term break from drama school.

I wanted to show the best parts of each of their ancestral lands, and since they all know their countries better than I ever would, it just made sense to bring all the Traditional Owners into the conversation.

I remember Rosemary Blight and I meeting the CEO and Chairs of the Jawoyn Association and Nitmulak Tours—John Berto, Lisa Mumbin and Jane Runyu—to tell them what the film was about and asking if they were okay with us shooting on country in Katherine Gorge. I was so adamant in assuring them we would be incredibly safe and respectful on their lands and Lisa cheekily asked, 'Yeah sure, who's your co-star? What does he look like?' I showed Lisa and Jane a picture of Gwilym and they began to fan themselves in jest, saying, 'Oh, we're definitely coming to set!' Once we asked everyone, that was it. We were never turned away by any of the Traditional Owners. I'm sure it would have been different if we were making a film about a serial murderer or giant croc, but it just goes to show that so much drama gets out of the way if you just ask. I was so grateful for the generous spirit and welcome that was given to the film and the crew wherever we went.

Luckily they all saw that Josh Tyler and I had written a love letter to the Territory, and because they shared a bit of their knowledge with us, the NT became more than the heat, crocs and cyclones.

As the shoot progressed I felt so proud that audiences who saw the film would have a chance to understand why the Territory is so important to Lauren (the bride-to-be) because they were given a window into cultures that span beyond 65,000 years—the cultures that celebrate how special that part of the world is and why it is worth protecting.

CHAPTER ELEVEN

THANKS, MS JACKSON

WHAT IS THAT SAYING? 'YOU WANT SOMETHING DONE, ask a busy person.' Well, I was definitely getting things done. And I was loving every minute of it. I arrived back in Australia after the eating-drinking-catching-up-with-friends-spending-time-with-James best holiday ever and I had two weeks to learn my role in *Black is the New White*. I had never performed the play before, but thankfully I'd had an absolute ball watching it at the Sydney Theatre Company back in its first season. I already knew that my friend Nakkiah was an incredible comedy writer from that and her work in the ABC's *Black Comedy*, but I still wasn't ready for the spell the play would cast on me.

The play follows Charlotte Gibson, a hardworking Aboriginal lawyer who falls head over heels for a struggling cello player, Francis Smith. At first the audience is led to believe her parents won't be thrilled when their daughter brings the whitest boy ever home for Christmas, but it's when Francis's father, Dennison Smith, bursts through the front door that you realise there is another connection happening here. It turns out that Dennison already knows Charlotte's father, Ray Gibson. And they don't only know each other, they despise each other. Ray is 'the handsome, charismatic Aboriginal politician with a great head of hair, who at one point was being touted as the future leader of the Labor party'. His political rival back in the nineties was Dennison Smith, 'the dour, conservative Social Services Minister, who wore very expensive suits and had ambitions for the prime ministership that were supported by no one'.

I was about to play Charlotte's sister, Rose, a successful fashion designer based in LA who is married to rugby star Sonny Jones. Rose is quite staunch about Aboriginal women continuing the Black lineage by having babies with an Aboriginal partner. All of the characters have strong opinions on race, class and privilege—the things you try to avoid discussing with family members at Christmas time—which makes it incredibly hard for Francis and Charlotte to stay together. The year before, a Nyoongar actor, Kylie Farmer (now Bracknell), had played Rose, and she got that Kardashian–LA vibe down pat. But Kylie had now fallen pregnant and would be too close to the due date to play Rose this time around, which is why I got the call from the director Paige Rattray. My friend Anthony Taufa was playing Sonny. He had been in Shari's year at NIDA—the year below me. When I had seen the show in Sydney I'd been very confused at first as to why my friend, who was Tongan, was playing an Aboriginal man. I didn't know what to think. But then, as the play goes on, we find out that Sonny appeared in a TV show called *Where Do You Come From?*, where they trace back the person's ancestral past. After Rose and Charlotte have a big row (which turns into a hilariously savage food fight) the DNA test comes back to reveal that Sonny is actually Tongan—like Anthony. I felt like such an idiot for letting Nakkiah fool me like this—I had just been utterly consumed by Christmas joy and love. Mariah's 'All I Want for Christmas Is You' kicks off the second half, and I was beside myself with happiness, dancing and singing along to the lyrics. It was the wonderful Luke Carroll's job to get everyone up to clap and dance in the aisles. He plays the narrator and 'Spirit of Christmas' in the show, and I had a front-row seat when I saw the play (thankfully I didn't get covered in food) and was pulled up on stage to dance with the cast. I honestly had the most magical time. It was a rom-com written by my bestie, so I lost myself in the magic and completely forgot where I was. All my friends were in the play and I adored them even more seeing them as this family. I had completely embarrassed them with my loud laughing and cheering—everyone in the audience kept looking around to see who was carrying on like they were at their child's school concert. But I couldn't help it. I was like a proud mum.

So, now it was having another run, and I was incredibly intimidated by joining this tight-knit cast. Most of the other actors had got the hang of all the timings and delivery of the lines. It was almost as if I were about to memorise a dance routine everyone else had already learned by heart. Which meant that it was going to be challenging physically and mentally. Timing is everything. I had asked James to help me with the lines but some of the ideas were so big that I wondered if two weeks was going to be enough for me to get this all right. I have a terrible habit of putting pressure on myself. I knew the genre intimately enough to understand the world we were in, so I had to have faith in my abilities. I wasn't alone in this rehearsal process, either. A lovely Perth actor, Tom Stokes, was newly cast as Francis Smith, so at least we could share our nervousness.

The valuable things I learned from performing in *Black is the New White* put me in good stead for *Top End Wedding*, especially the art of reacting at the same time as delivering a line. With most dramatic acting a lot of strong facial expressions are pulled before you say the line—but there was no room for that kind of air in this play. It was also an opportunity for me to remind myself what it takes for comedy to really sing, which was important because our shooting schedule for the film was going to be incredibly ambitious (we had six weeks to shoot the whole thing—which is about a quarter of the time actors spend working on an American blockbuster). I was grateful that Goalpost could accommodate me performing in *Black is the New White* but unfortunately pre-production fell across the last leg of the tour. Normally theatre companies in Australia don't allow actors to leave halfway through a tour, but this time they were willing to make an exception.

While I was in Wollongong doing the play, Liam Heyen, one of the co-producers from Goalpost, was trying to get clearance to use Janet Jackson's song 'Escapade' in the film. I had been a bit cheeky and thrown in songs that I loved in

I am incredibly close to my parents. I get my Larrakia and Tiwi blood from
my mother. I get my Irish Roman Catholic heritage from my father.
I have never had anything but love and care from both sides of my family.

My training at NIDA has been one of the reasons I've thrived. This photo is from the dress rehearsal of the NIDA production of *Antony and Cleopatra* in 2007 (before I fell off the stage).

As a young actor I was so thankful for the chance to act in Belvoir St Theatre's production of *Yibiyung*. This photo is of me with the remarkable David Page, an inspiring, creative and talented actor, composer and entertainer.

(Thank you to Stephen Page for permission to reproduce this photo. Image from Belvoir St Theatre, photograph by Heidrun Lohr.)

Wow! On the Cannes Film Festival red carpet with Shari Sebbens, Jessica Mauboy, Wayne Blair and Deborah Mailman.

LEFT TO RIGHT: Chris O'Dowd, Deborah Mailman, Shari Sebbens, Jessica Mauboy and me. *The Sapphires* was an incredible experience and working with these vibrant, talented and inspiring women will always be a highlight of my career.

LEFT: With my gorgeous *Love Child* colleagues, Harriet Dyer and Sophie Hensser.
RIGHT: Winning a Logie for the role of Martha Tennant was wonderful. Winning two
was pretty remarkable. Seizing the moment to talk from my heart ... Priceless.

LEFT: Origin loser. Me with Andy Ryan. This anguish went on for years. RIGHT: Introducing
Playschool's new Indigenous doll, Kiya, to Australian children was a big deal. Working
with Hunter Page-Lochard and Luke Carroll to celebrate country and culture gives me
hope. For Black kids, watching 'themselves' on TV as part of positive everyday portrayals
makes a big difference to a sense of self and a sense of belonging.

My girlfriends are my sisters. I can't imagine life without them. Not all are in the industry but Shari Sebbens (top), another Darwin girl, is a kindred spirit. She started at NIDA when I was in my second year and I have been lucky enough to work with this awesome woman many times. This photo was taken when we were both appearing in Nakkiah Lui's play, *Black is the New White*. Speaking of Nakkiah (bottom left), what a magnificent woman she is! Working with her and the two Kates (bottom right), Kate McCartney and Kate McLennan, on *Get Krack!n's* final episode of season two was an extraordinary opportunity to put a spotlight on the way First Nations people have been let down.

I was focusing on work, being single and writing *Top End Wedding* when I met James Colley – and it was like I had conjured my perfect partner off the page. James helps ground me, supports me and even came with me when I sought out the door from the movie *Notting Hill* and emulated Bridget Jones in the UK snow. Marrying James was such a special day.

LEFT: Filming on Tiwi was so special. I got to be with family and felt so embraced and cared for. RIGHT: Gwilym and me with my cousins, Joseph and Kadeem, who are Kakadu National Park Rangers, during filming.

ABOVE LEFT: With my onscreen grandparents, Bernard and Lynette.

ABOVE RIGHT: Josh and me during filming. I don't think either of us could quite believe our story was being made.

LEFT: Together with James, Mum and Dad at the Adelaide premiere of Top End Wedding.

LEFT: Showing the film at the 2019 Sundance Film Festival in Utah was a BIG deal. From left to right: Murray Lui, Gwilym Lee, Joshua Tyler, me and Wayne Blair. RIGHT: New York – yellow cab, Lincoln Center, a Toni Matičevski gown– yes, a place where dreams definitely do come true!

Living away from the Territory means that I don't get to be in constant connection with language and culture, but I like to think that creating *Top End Wedding* was my way of keeping something alive within me that I will carry always.

the big print of the script. If you've never read a screenplay before, the big print is just the setting of the scene before the characters speak. So, I would often put down a song that I envisaged would play around the brief description of where the characters are and what they're doing. Along with Janet Jackson, I added some of my favourite music from the NT— Electric Fields, B2M, Nabarlek band and Emily Wurramara, among others. Goalpost were told by Sony that Ms Jackson was understandably very protective of her music, so we had to be prepared for her to say no. Liam had called to ask if I could write to her so she would see how connected I was to this story.

So, as a silly fan girl, I wrote her this.

Dear Janet Jackson,

Re: ESCAPADE

I am writing to you for permission to have your wonderful song 'Escapade' in the film I co-wrote called *Top End Wedding*. As a proud Australian Aboriginal woman, I grew up loving your music. The film follows a young bride-to-be called Lauren, who I will play. She is engaged to Ned and they have travelled to the Australian outback where Lauren grew up for their wedding. Lauren and her bridesmaids hear 'Escapade' come on when they are out on the town for her hen's night. They squeal with excitement and reminisce about their high school years by repeating the choreography they learned watching the music video on TV. After many years of living away in Sydney, it's about uptight Lauren letting go of all the restraints that the city life brings and allowing herself to be present with her family and the man she loves.

Your music brings so much joy to the Aboriginal men and women I know, and I know that when they hear the first few bars of the song, they would be dancing in the movie theatre.

Australian Aboriginal people hold so much solidarity with the African–American community that we can't help but enjoy the stories and music that many African–American artists like yourself make.

I want not only Aboriginal people, but many First Nations and people of colour to see themselves in this romantic comedy, and realise that they are worthy of love and happiness.

Warmest regards,

Miranda

With bated breath, we waited to hear back. In the meantime, I was told I would have to look for another song in case 'Escapade' was rejected. For the run of the play, Shari and I shared a dressing room, and she started suggesting some bangers. The problem was that the nineties was the era of the slow jams. There was plenty of girl power around to show the connection between these best friends, but I wanted something as upbeat as 'Escapade'.

On my last night on *Black is the New White*, we had a big group hug to send me off and wish me well. Nakkiah took over as Rose for the Parramatta and Canberra legs of the tour and I headed up to Darwin to start pre-production on *Top End Wedding*.

There was so much to be done that I almost (almost but not quite) forgot about the song-permission question. Thankfully, Liam called to let me know that Ms Jackson had read my letter herself (*Aaaagh!!!!*). Then it turned out, not only had Janet Jackson taken the time to read my letter, she had said that I could play her song in my movie! I was on cloud nine. Now we just had to make the movie.

Normally writers don't go along with crew to look at different locations to shoot, but because I knew the Top End so well, I went up. I stayed at my parents' house, which was right around the corner from where the rest of the crew were staying. In the week we were there, Cyclone Marcus hit town. Many storms have wreaked havoc across the city over the years. Cyclone Tracy was the most infamous of all, arriving on Christmas morning in 1974 and causing the most damage, killing seventy-one people and obliterating most of Darwin. But many others have packed a punch, including Thelma, Ingrid and Monica. I appreciated that in more recent times cyclones had been called male names such as Paul, Carlos and Grant; it just seems more fitting with all the damage the patriarchy has done to let the males take the rap.

While Cyclone Marcus wasn't quite strong enough to lift cows up into the stratosphere like in *Twister*, the severity of the winds still uprooted many trees across the city and took down powerlines. It wasn't particularly safe for us to go and look for locations while the storm raged itself out. Despite the fact that most offices and businesses had closed due to the severity of the cyclone, my poor cousin Talisha, a hairdresser, still had to work. Talisha had only just got her licence and so was understandably very intimidated by the idea of driving in the unpredictable weather but she didn't want to disappoint clients.

It was all a bit wacky, really. Even if Talisha and the other hairdressers were safe indoors, why would anyone choose to get their hair done only for it to be ruined in the cyclonic wind and rain? To make matters worse, Talisha texted her mother once she got to work to say that the water wasn't even running in the studio, so they were using rain water they collected in buckets to wash out the hair dye in their clients' hair!

But storms are unpredictable and this one was getting worse, so Talisha's mother, Aunty Sonia, was worried. Since my parents live five minutes away from the salon, she called my mother to see if she could try to get Talisha out of this ridiculous (and possibly dangerous) situation. To Aunty Sonia's relief, my mother drove out in the wind and rain to get Talisha from work and then chaperoned her as she drove back to our place like a police vehicle would escort the American president's car.

With Talisha in lockdown with us, I took my chance. I am crap at styling my own hair, except for a ponytail or bun. So, while we were hiding out from the storm, I asked my cousin to teach me how to braid. Talisha made the mistake of offering her own hair to practise on. Needless to say, I probably pulled most of the hair out of the poor girl's scalp, but I am hoping that her pain was my gain.

After a while the storm quietened down and the boredom of no power and a cousin who kept asking for hair-grooming tips must have taken effect because Talisha decided to head home. The fact that powerlines were underground on Talisha's side of town and so the electricity would still be up and running there was probably a factor in her decision as well.

Fortunately for the film crew, their hotel had its own generators, so they had full power. My parents' house, on the other hand, was in complete blackout by the time the sun set. Not only were all the lights out, my parents' fancy induction stove was also out of order. But because MacGyver gave birth to me, my mother resorted to using their camping stove to cook food.

Most people with parents who grew up in low socio-economic housing will know how manic they get about waste. And, to be honest, the average household in Australia does waste too much. At the end of every term at my mother's primary school, my grandmother was employed to do a full clean of the classrooms. Because Nan didn't have a babysitter and cleaning the school was a massive task, she got her kids to help. My mum would tell me that when she was a kid she was constantly astounded by the amount of waste they would find when they were helping Nan. Mum would find uncut oranges and unopened muesli bars that kids had thrown away, and she would wash them to eat later. It was also where they got their pencils and other stationery for the next term. Growing up poor made my mum appreciate what she now had and she was adamant about eating the food she had in the fridge, like the short-lived TV show *Surprise Chef.* I really admire Mum's consciousness of waste, so I try to do the same. That night Dad had some white wine in the fridge, so Mum told us to drink it before it got too warm and vinegary. I liked that excuse. We sat eating whatever we had and drinking wine while surrounded by LED lights. It reminded me of camping out bush, and it was lovely. The truth is, Barbara Tapsell is prepared for the apocalypse. She has baked beans and batteries ready to go. While every other Darwinian was ravaging the aisles at Woolworths, my mum was tranquil at home, casually taping up her windows in case they were smashed by debris. 'A cyclone is a possibility every year,' she'd vent to me, shaking her head in disbelief. 'Why do people wait until crisis point to get their shit together?' Excellent question, Barbara!

By the second day of no power, the novelty of this Bear Grylls lifestyle had worn off. The rain had moved on, so the air was sticky. We opened up the windows to get some air flow, but we needed the fans on to make it bearable. It reminded me of why we save camping for the dry season. It was going to be at least another two nights until Mum and Dad's house would have any power. I wasn't going to last.

It turned out, we didn't have to. My parents and I ended up at the same hotel as the crew. Not only did I have the comfort of air-conditioning, I could finally chat to James. I had managed to text him the night before to let him know about my situation but then the phone battery went flat. I was also able to go online and learned that Cyclone Marcus was being reported as the worst natural disaster in Darwin since Cyclone Tracy.

A story in the *NT News* caught my eye. High school sweethearts Stephanie Hill and Joel Pavy were supposed to get married just as Cyclone Marcus was due to hit Darwin. When the storm moved closer the day before they decided to go ahead with the celebration, despite the ceremony being timed to begin just as the Bureau of Meteorology (BOM) predicted the cyclone would hit. It reminded me that we were on the right track with our film—we could be as outlandish as we wanted, because if two people can get married during a cyclone, then anything is possible.

The skies began to clear up and my parents got their power back—but Marcus had set us a day behind on our tech recce.

It meant we had a shorter time to look at all the locations, so everyone had to make quick decisions. Our first stop was Katherine. I met with the Jawoyn Traditional Owners again, with Rosemary. I had made strong points about creating a very transparent dialogue with every Traditional Owner whose land we were filming on, so I felt the need to set the example. The idea of engaging with Traditional Owners, especially when the film has an Indigenous gaze, is still a new concept for the Australian arts, so I took this meeting very seriously—especially when I didn't have any family in this community. I wore one of my nicest dresses, put on a pair of wedges, a touch of concealer and mascara. We were set up in their boardroom with nibbles, so I was ready to be incredibly formal. Rosemary had a PowerPoint presentation about the whole production to date that showed everything from the funding to the scheduling to all of the people involved in front of and behind the camera. Turns out, the Aunties just wanted a cup of tea and a chat. It's not that they didn't appreciate what we were sharing, but they said they knew I was a Territory girl, that I had been raised to be respectful and that I was proud of where I grew up. This trust was so important to me.

* * *

Jabiru had changed a lot since I had moved away in 2001. When I was growing up there, it had a real sense of community. If you worked at Jabiru like my parents, you lived in Jabiru. But Jabiru was built for the miners. Now that there was a fly-in–fly-out program for them, they could base their families in Darwin rather than Jabiru. Even though tourism would still flourish in Kakadu and the land where the mine was would be given back to the Mirarr, the population of Jabiru declined. But the beauty of Kakadu was not lost. Is it incredibly dorky to be proud of where you grew up? It was exciting for me to show people who had never come up to the Territory the magic of the place.

I was especially excited to take the crew to Nourlangie Rock, a place known for its ancient rock art. 'Namarrgon the Lightning Man' is the most famous painting there. With stone axes on his knees and elbows, he is Black Thor. He is a significant creation, ancestor to the Mirarr people, who believe that he is the story behind Kakadu's intense thunderstorms.

Before going on the tech recce, I had read that the journal *Nature* was the first to report that archaeologists had gone to an ancient camp site near Jabiluka Mine in Kakadu with Mirarr elders and had found a stone axe close to 80,000 years old. This discovery meant that archaeologists had to recalibrate how long they believed the Traditional Owners have been living on this land. I was touched that the people involved in this project were able to see a culture and a history that is special, and worth knowing and learning about.

Every place we visited on that recce was a place I was proud to introduce the others to. I had already been to Tiwi a few times but I needed the community to meet the people who would work behind the camera on our film. When we arrived, one of the older ladies in the Wangatunga Strong Women Choir, Leoni, marched up to the car and demanded, 'What you mob doing here?' My heart leaped into my throat. Were we disrespecting her? Did someone forget to tell her? And would this matriarch give the movie a bad name before we had even begun? All my fears rushed into my brain. Had we not been transparent with the community? Had I let them all down? Luckily, I was being melodramatic and our production coordinator Libby stepped forward and told her Aunty in Tiwi that the crew were here for the yimanka (film). The old lady gave a big laugh and said, 'Oh yeah, I forgot!' Phew!

One thing we needed to do on this trip was cast Lauren's grandparents, and Wayne, the director, wanted me to meet with the people he had in mind, Bernard and Lynette. I was incredibly touched when Bernard said to me, 'I really hope this film makes people here, particularly the young people, see how important it is to learn old Tiwi from us. I go to all the schools to tell students this. I tell them if they don't learn to speak it, if they only talk new Tiwi, it will go with us. But it doesn't reach them. So, maybe if they see it in a movie, they will understand this better.' This broke my heart to hear, but I was soothed by his belief that the film would do this for the community.

Wayne decided to film their audition at the old church at Wurrumiyanga, which is where I had my heart set on having Lauren and Ned's wedding. Even though it's no longer where the local devout Catholics worship on Sunday, they still open it up for weddings and christenings. This gorgeous weatherboard church survived being blown up by Japanese pilots in 1942 and being blown away by Cyclone Tracy in 1974. I couldn't think of a more sturdy and resilient church to be a metaphor for a commitment like Lauren and Ned's. Or Trevor and Daffy's (Lauren's parents), for that matter.

For the audition, Libby stepped in as Daffy, while I played Lauren. Wayne had essentially told Bernard and Lynette the plot of the film and encouraged them to say whatever they wanted in old Tiwi. It just had to be welcoming and loving towards Daffy and Lauren. Then, out of nowhere, Bernard became Robert Redford. A bloody Hollywood movie star. He was just luminous. His eyes sparkled when he referred to Libby as his daughter. He put his hand on his heart, as if it had just burst out of his chest. Then he gently took Libby's face in his hands, almost in disbelief that she was there in front of him. After he kissed the top of her head, his soft face brightened as he smiled. He gave me the biggest bear hug I've ever been given. Libby translated what Bernard was saying to us both afterwards, and I got goosebumps. This man was an absolute poet, saying things like, 'My heart is so full to see you again, my daughter. I've missed you. I'm very happy that you are back here on your country.' I could barely keep it together. We had our grandparents.

Our whole time on Tiwi land was magical. For the first time, I learned the dance of my Totem, the Jungle Fowl (more widely known as the Orange-Footed Scrub Fowl). It was so lovely to be taught by the women in the choir. They were all talking over the top of each other explaining the moves I had to learn. As they clapped to the beat and sang, it was as if this gap in my soul, this longing I'd never understood or been able to express, had been filled. Liam filmed the dance so I could look back on it and remember it for the shoot. The ladies couldn't contain their excitement, and when one suggested that I wear tapalingini (a feather and reed headdress) the rest all chimed in and mentioned the pamijini (armbands) on both arms. I was slightly melancholy at the thought that I hadn't learned this as a child, but I was thankful to be learning it now.

We only had a few weeks before the shoot was scheduled to begin, so there wasn't time for me to go back to Melbourne. I flew to Adelaide for the start of pre-production, where I was picked up from the airport and taken straight to a costume fitting. I could not believe it was all coming together. I'm aware that many filmmakers work for at least a decade before they witness their film go into production, but here we were, not even four years after the spark of an idea that Josh and I had first created. It was quite surreal to see every element of the story come to life off the page and to talk about the practicalities of making my vision a reality. Our costume designer, Heather Wallace, had put together wonderful outfits for all the lead cast. I asked for my wedding dress to be made in a full Tiwi print. It was quite pricey for the tiny costume budget because it was screen-printed satin that had to be shipped from an isolated town—but I had envisioned this dress very clearly when I was writing the wedding scenes with Josh and I knew that it would be the thing that would tell the audience they hadn't been transported to just any Aboriginal community. There is nothing that irritates me more than when

I tell people I'm from Darwin and they talk about their time in Alice Springs or Arnhem Land. They are not the same. I was fifteen the last time I was in Arnhem Land. I'd only ever been in Alice Springs for a week. Comparing them all is like telling a Parisian you share common ground with them because you've been to Monaco. Don't waste anyone's time with that. I wanted the audience to know they were on the Tiwi Islands, and Heather knew how much this meant to me.

The look of the film was coming together. I knew all the lines but still had to learn the dance routine—choreographed by Leanne Scott-Toms—for the 'Escapade' scene. (Thank you again, Janet!) I wanted the dance between Lauren and her girlfriends to be like they had memorised it from *Rage* or *MTV*. Shari Sebbens, Elaine Crombie and Dalara Williams had come across from Sydney to practise with me. I had told Heather that these were girls who knew how to dress to impress, so they needed to be off-the-charts glamorous in their costuming. We needed to honour their beauty in this film.

I am incredibly insecure about choreography. I know that dance is a useful skill for an actor—since it's the same part of the brain you have to use when a director has told you to walk and talk somewhere the camera is positioned—but when the music starts and someone yells, 'Five, six, seven, eight!'

it's intimidating to me. I'm just not confident in the dance department. I wish I could twerk but I have no junk to throw around in the trunk.

Thankfully, the gym at our hotel had tall mirrors. Since barely anyone used it, I went all out. I would go through the steps first thing in the morning. I was determined to honour Janet's song and not stuff it up.

But dancing wasn't the only way I had to stretch myself for this role. The biggest rookie move I made as a first-time screenwriter was to create a lead character who speaks fluent French. I *do not* speak fluent French. In my defence, not only am I overconfident as hell, it was to make a point of Lauren being so disconnected from her own culture that she has chosen to embrace a second language from a Western culture before engaging with her own. It was incredibly stupid of me to not have thought this through but thankfully one of the producers, Kate Croser, brought her mother—a French teacher—to the hotel to help me with my pronunciation. Although I was only saying a few words, I had been cramming in all the French I could in the weeks before shooting: I was playing Duolingo (the language learning app) and listening and repeating words from French audiobooks. I was envious how accessible learning the language was; there are many more French speakers than

Tiwi. It made me sad, and I wished I lived in a country that encouraged Aboriginal languages to be spoken more fluently in schools. Without that, Bernard is right, we are going to lose important languages. Making this film gave us the chance to help record Tiwi before it is potentially lost forever.

CHAPTER TWELVE

GOING HOME

IT WAS FINALLY HAPPENING. AFTER SEVENTEEN YEARS OF dreaming, this little Black girl from the Territory was finally starring in a lead role. And it was one she had written herself! She was going back to her hometown and sharing this with her family and the friends who had seen her leave everything that made her comfortable in order to chase this. The dream had come true. I was missing James back home in Melbourne, but it meant the world to me knowing how much he supported me in this.

The night before our first day of filming, Gwilym had left me a bottle of sparkling wine and a lovely card thanking me for writing this story with Josh. It reminded me how special it was to finally be making this heartwarming film, one through which people would get to see everything that goes right in an Aboriginal community, in some of the most isolated places in the country. The cast and crew had been brought together to make this come to life. To top it all off, because I had just watched clips from my queen Beyoncé's performance at Coachella, which had gone viral on social media that weekend, I was completely amped.

For me, the first day of shooting felt like Christmas Day. We were parked in Victoria Square in the middle of Adelaide. My heart felt incredibly full to have Karl Telfer, a local Kaurna man, welcome us to his ancestors' land. Starting the filming outside of the Territory made me feel like a foreigner, but I felt safe and content knowing that we had the guidance of the people who knew this area intimately.

My first scene was ridiculous. Everything had to come together so quickly that, naturally, I was quite nervous. James keeps reminding me that even though I'm a nerd and over-prepare, I process what I'm doing through a state of anxiety. Understanding this means I have learned not to psych myself out so much, but the nerves are still there.

Josh had written a scene in which Lauren eats a pastry and all the fine caster sugar it is coated with goes all over her black suit. Right before she is due to meet clients. Wayne suggested that I use a chair to try to wipe off the caster sugar. Like I've said before, comedy is quite a dance. I pushed a breath out of my nostrils as I took a ridiculously big bite out of this pastry, sending caster sugar everywhere. Also, when Lauren's boss, Ellen Hampton, entered the room, I snapped the heel of my stiletto and tried to hide my limp. I think it helped that I couldn't hear the crew cackling behind Wayne's monitor, because I would have wanted to appeal to them rather than zoning in on the task at hand. Even though I know I'm aware people are watching, I become less self-conscious if I pretend they aren't there. I really only got two takes for each shot, but being a perfectionist I sometimes asked for a third. It made me realise just how technical comedic acting is. I think it also helped that Kerry Fox is the master of straight-faced acting, the way she looked at me during the scene made me want to pee myself.

This was also the big day that I had to display Lauren's French. I was so thankful that Kate's mum had helped me, because while I still don't speak French fluently, I at least got to a point where I was comfortable with pronouncing the words I had to say. I'm sure French speakers will be outraged when they watch it but I think I managed to make it sound

conversational rather than, 'Look at me speak French.' This
was a valuable lesson to learn.

After I got past my first-day nerves I realised—I got to be
Meg Ryan!

It was very beneficial for me that filming started in Adelaide.
Obviously it was what was going to work for everyone, but now
that I was acting, I really liked starting from the beginning of
the script. It meant that I could remind myself of who Lauren
was and remember her dynamic with Ned. It had been roughly
four months since I'd met Gwilym for the first time, and it
had been only for forty-five minutes.

Do you know why actors from Australia do so well in
Hollywood? It's because not only are we inundated with film
and television from England and America (so we've developed
the ear for those accents), we also only get two takes to get it
right. I would have loved to have made a blooper reel for this
film but had I messed up my lines the way so many actors
get to in any Hollywood comedy, I would have been 'that
wanker' who wasted everyone's time and money. No one on
an Australian film set finds multiple falling-over-laughing
mistakes charming in any way. The amount of time actors
have to bond on a Hollywood set is so foreign to me. Every
actor has to build that trust with others, but time is a luxury.

The industry is so small in Australia that you do have the advantage of knowing many of the actors before working with them. But Gwilym lived on the other side of the world, so we didn't get to hang out in the lead-up to shooting.

We had to be really comfortable with each other from the get-go, and I was thankful that Gwilym was such a kind dude since we didn't have a lot of time to get to know each other. I'm not the first actor to say that doing anything remotely romantic with another actor is similar to learning a dance routine. You end up talking through all the steps and often ask one another along the way, 'Is it okay if I put my hand on your knee?' or 'Can I kiss your neck?' and the like. There'll always be moments when you feel awkward, because you're having to be intimate with someone you aren't normally intimate with. But you can't go in to a role half-hearted, because you have to be believed. Basically, actors are professional liars. We are paid to trick you into thinking we are our characters.

Now, this isn't going to be popular with people from Adelaide but ... I actually like Port Adelaide. Don't judge me! It looks like a very quaint seaside town, and city people need to stop turning their noses up at those on the other side of a river to them! Also, blame Wayne for picking the apartment to shoot in for Ned and Lauren's home. It was a really modern loft that had a gorgeous big kitchen with the walls covered in lots of unusual art. I loved how worldly it made Lauren and Ned seem.

It was a wonderful feeling to watch the words Josh and I had written turn into a whole, real world. I was so grateful that we were finally underway. It's like getting into a cold pool: you can stand at the edge all day fretting about it but at some point you just have to jump in.

Despite having acted professionally for ten years, I had never before been part of a feature film writing process or seen an idea move all the way from concept to the real thing. Actors come in at the very last moment to sweep up all the credit. But this production was different. We had all worked so hard for so long to get to this day and finally our 'Christmas' had arrived.

At this point, I could finally relax into the role and be confident in what we had all put together. All I had to focus on now was being an actor and performing to the best of my ability.

It was frantic, of course. As I said earlier, we only had six weeks to shoot a whole film, and we had a lot of ground to cover. But once we were rolling, there was no time to stop. Next thing I knew, I blinked and we were in Darwin.

* * *

I was over the moon to be back on Larrakia country.

To be honest, I become a little cocky when I'm back on country. Suddenly I feel as if I can say or do whatever I want. You're in *my* house, baby! Obviously, I still have to respect elders and my mum is always ready to give me a clip over the ear if I get out of line, but anyone who is younger than me? Forget about it.

I felt invincible, knowing that the strength and resilience of my ancestors were connected to this soil. My younger cousin Kiarra welcomed the crew and cast to country. I know how much it takes for any young woman, but particularly young Aboriginal women, to speak in front of a crowd. Society conditions us to be invisible. A saying that has always stayed with me is one that my friend Melodie Reynolds-Diarra shared with me: 'Always treat non-Indigenous people like a visitor.'

There's an opportunity there, too. It's not all about who is in charge. It was so special for me to be able to welcome people in and share the wonders of my country with them. While I have deep connections with people in the big cities like Melbourne and Sydney, part of me feels like people know me better when they see me on Larrakia soil. That's the real me. It's where I'm most comfortable and where I like who I am. It's home.

I was excited for the next part of filming to be starting here. Thanks to the Indigenous Department at Screen Australia, the production had attached Aboriginal interns to the film—Heath Baxter, Sean Bahr-Kelly, Rachael Chisholm, John Hodgson and Elliana Lawford. Most of these mob grew up in Darwin, Tennant Creek and Alice Springs, so not only were they Territory people like me, they were passionate artists deserving of the opportunity.

One of the best parts about being back in Darwin was that it meant shooting with my girls. These three brilliantly talented comedic actresses, Shari Sebbens, Elaine Crombie and Dalara Williams, were playing Lauren's bridesmaids, and I couldn't have been happier that Wayne had cast women I had long relationships with and considered close friends. It was important that the audience felt like these girls had Lauren's back and that the group had the easy rapport that only comes from old friendships. The girls had to represent the safety net of being home and the cost of leaving, even if Lauren wasn't aware of it at first.

Shari is a Darwin kid like me, and she has always been a great comfort to me wherever we are in the world. It's nice sometimes to share your homesickness with someone who can truly understand. There are people who carry their home with them wherever they go, and when you talk with them you feel as if you're home, too. Shari does that. Whenever I felt lost or overwhelmed living in a big city I could turn to Shari and know that I wasn't alone.

So, filming with my girlfriends was going to be fun. We had been working our butts off on the choreography for Lauren's big hen's night dance and all of a sudden it was time to do it for real. Staying true to the rom-com world we were building, we needed a song that connected the main character and her best friend. It's a quick way to show friendship between women. Also, I just love throwing it down and I'm not going to apologise for it.

It was true to life, too. When we were kids, my cousins and I used to build our own dance routines, copying moves from *Rage* in the mornings. It was that nostalgia I hoped to capture, to allow filmgoers to see these women as young girls, in their lounge room, trying to be just like Janet. And, to be fair, Janet is beloved by Aboriginal and Torres Strait Islander women, so it made sense. I had certainly danced my legs down to my knees to Janet in all my high school dance classes.

We were shooting in Darwin's perfectly named gay club, Throb. It is famous in Darwin, renowned for its incredible drag shows and endlessly fun atmosphere. While it was a lovely and safe space for LGBTQI people to be their most authentic selves, it was also without a doubt the best place to go partying in Darwin. Those two things colliding isn't a coincidence.

I was thrilled that Wayne had chosen that location and was stunned by what the art department had done. They must have bought out all the party decorations from every Kmart in the area!

Our choreographer, Leanne, was there to walk us through the steps one more time to make sure we got it right. It was also a big crowd scene, which gave me a chance to sneak a few family members into the background. That wasn't just for a shot of fame but a chance to show them what I actually do for a living. Acting is such a strange job to have, and I think a lot of the time my family and friends might think I'm rude when I don't answer a message during the day, especially my mum who will threaten to call the federal police if she hasn't heard from me within a certain timeframe. But when they finally saw me in a work environment and saw how frantically things move, I think they understood a bit better and appreciated that I don't ignore anyone, I am just always short on time.

That was the added benefit of this film: the opportunity for me to show my family that just because I'm away from

Darwin a lot of the time doesn't mean I don't think about them. It was important for me to show them not only how much my dreams meant to me but that they were part of those dreams, too.

We shot for six days across the week in Darwin, so when we finally had our one day off, Rose organised a bus to take us out to Buley Rockhole, where we had shot our original trailer and where Rex thought—incorrectly, as I mentioned—that he got bitten by a snake. Shari got everyone together, and we took champagne, cheese, dips and crackers to picnic there for the day.

The swimming hole was packed with locals and tourists. Gwilym and I met a guy who was spending the day with his wife and son at Buley. He had recognised me and asked what we were doing out there, and when I told him we were making a film called *Top End Wedding* he said, 'I've got the sequel for you: *Top End Divorce*. Come to my place to get a few tips.' He said this all within earshot of his wife and kid. All I could manage to say was, 'Righto,' and we moved on.

There was also a local rugby team at the swimming hole. We were sitting and watching as one of them was dared to dack himself. He leaped at the opportunity and started to twirl his, uh, toodoi around like a tassel as his friends cheered him on. And, to top it all off, one of them had lost their grip and dropped a can of unopened cider into the water. Gwilym reached out and managed to grab it before it could slip into the current, raising it above his head for another cheer from the rugby boys. Welcome to Darwin, mate!

The trip might not have been as tranquil as I would have liked on our only day off, but Buley Rockhole is one of my favourite places on earth and nothing can spoil my mood when I'm swimming out in that water on Kungarakan country.

But there's no rest for the wicked, so next thing we knew we were packing up and heading out on the ferry to Tiwi.

* * *

There was a buzz in the air as we reached our destination to shoot the wedding. We had been waiting for this moment for so long. This was the heart of the film, so I was incredibly excited when we all arrived. The crew and cast were treated like rock stars when we touched Tiwi soil. And I held so many babies it was ridiculous.

We shot a couple of scenes with my Uncle Jason, whose alter ego, as I mentioned, is Foxxy Empire. So, Uncle Foxxy. Uncle Foxxy had improvised so many great lines, it was hard not to break out of character by laughing. Okay, I did laugh. I did break out of character. I blame my uncle. In the scene where Lauren is driven on a motorbike across town with her uncle to meet all the mob. Murray Lui, the director of photography, was being driven behind us to film while Foxxy and I drove past all the locals waving at us. Again, it's crazy that some people wanted this cut out of the script. How does anyone care about two people getting married if you don't see how invested the family and friends are in their love and life?

It was like we were on Tiwi for an actual wedding. In fact, lots of older Tiwi mob believed there *was* a wedding happening. I heard from others that Libby had to save Gwilym from my grandmother's grasp because she was giving him the third degree. I can imagine it was along the lines of, 'If you break my granddaughter's heart, you'll have me to deal with.' This is my own fault. When I'd tried to get James over to the Island two years earlier, there were cyclones forming off the coast of Broome in Western Australia. While it was safe to go over, had the cyclone hit the Islands we may have been stuck there for a week or four, depending on the weather. I thought it was best we stayed on the mainland, so James had never been to the Tiwi Islands.

When we weren't filming, I wasn't at the social club with the rest of the crew because I was too busy teaching my mum and Aunty the steps to the Jungle Fowl dance. They had come across to be extras in the wedding scene, which was happening the next day. I could tell that Mum wasn't thrilled with the short time she had to learn the moves, because she was in a huff and kept asking for the video to be repeated. I tried to be encouraging, but Mum was also resigned to the fact that I had done high school dance so of course I would pick up choreography faster. According to my mother, I might as well be the principal dancer at Bangarra. It can be very hard to convince her she can do something once she's made her mind up she can't. I don't know how many people in her life have reminded her how capable she truly is, so I make the effort to not lose my patience with her in these times.

After rehearsal, Mum, Dad and Aunty Maur dropped me back at the accommodation, where everyone had come back from the social club. These women could not contain their excitement and they began to sing a song they had just written for Lauren, about welcoming her back home to family and to country. I could not hold my tears back. Even though I couldn't fully understand what they were singing, it was from a place of deep longing and love. I looked over at

Gwilym and I could see how touched he was by this song too. When they finished, he came over and spoke about how the Welsh sang with the same spirit. How special that must have been for him.

The next day, the excitement had become contagious. The wedding was on. No matter how many times people were told that it was all pretend, no one wanted their bubble to burst. They were at my wedding.

It was hot, and I had forgotten how satin doesn't breathe in heat. But beauty is pain, and I felt gorgeous in the dress Heather had made for me. The dressmaker had done an incredible job making sure the print wasn't lost in the sewing. I made sure to capture many photos of me in it. I was so thrilled that Josh was there as well: he had come over especially for the wedding scene. I really didn't want him to miss this.

I was a little overwhelmed by it all, because many of my family were still under the impression it was my actual wedding. But filming takes time. The Western Bulldogs and the Hawthorn Hawks were playing that day, and a few of their hard-core fans were keen to leave to watch the game. Not only that, the older ladies in the choir were starting to get hot and tired. People's focus was waning and they couldn't understand why the ceremony was taking so long. Bless, they had never been to a film set, and they didn't think they were even on one. To keep the footy fans happy, Libby had to keep running into the church between takes to tell everyone the score.

I was thrilled to have local Tiwi star Rob Collins play the priest for Lauren and Gwilym's wedding. Rob had already played the villain in *Cleverman* and the romantic lead in *The Wrong Girl* but now he was back home, playing a man of the cloth. He was finally reining himself in and living a humble life. The Aunties couldn't resist teasing him!

In the film, as Ned's brother Robbie is left to occupy the people and stall the wedding while Ned is trying to get over to the Island on a little motorboat, he asks the guests, 'Anyone got any jokes?' The camera was on my dad at this point and he burst out laughing and said, 'Oh, that's a really great line!' like he was at the theatre. Wayne had to run over and tell him that he couldn't laugh because everyone had to appear displeased at waiting so long. So unprofessional, Tone.

It felt bizarre to walk down the aisle as a character before I had walked down the aisle as myself. It was especially weird because this was going to happen for real for James and me in six months' time. I would have loved James to have been here to see this. We tried in vain to bring him up. He even joked about saying our vows right after Wayne called 'cut' in the church to save some wedding costs. Sadly his demanding work schedule wouldn't allow it. Especially when it would take him two days at the very least to get over here. But he was there in spirit.

During this scene, Aunty Maur actually cried, and she wasn't aware that Murray Lui captured her on film. This Aunty would always travel down with my cousins Denay and Caleb to Sydney to see the plays I was in. Caleb is only three weeks younger than me, and when we were kids Aunty Maur and Mum often helped each other out with the raising of the two of us—sorry, separating us when we fought with each other. Aunty Maur wears her heart on her sleeve. Poor thing, how was she going to be on the actual day? Mum told me she asked her sister, 'Maureen, you know she's not getting married today?' She said, 'I know, but she just looks so beautiful.' Bless my second mum.

But as my eyes met Gwilym's, I felt an unspoken gratitude between the two of us. I had made myself incredibly vulnerable in front of him with this story—he had met my community and he had been on my ancestral lands. I was showing this man I hardly knew a huge piece of my heart because I would not be who I am without either of those things. As bloody humiliating and scary as that can feel, you have to put yourself in those positions all the time as a creative person if you want to make the kind of art that speaks to people. I would not be doing what I am doing today without the teachings of family and country. I still have a lot to learn, of course, but I always feel like the best version of myself when I remember who I am. While we still had Kakadu and Katherine to go, I put my trust in Gwilym and he didn't take lightly how much this film meant to me, and for that I will be forever thankful.

Mixing reality with make-believe is never easy, and a lot of the old people tried to eat the prop food. The crew had to keep telling them that, 1) it could make them sick given it had been sitting there for hours and, 2) lunch was coming soon.

When we finally stopped for our real lunch I enjoyed a bit of relief from the satin. The old women from the choir got a second wind and started singing again, their beautiful voices lifting everyone's spirits. Then it was time for the women to do the Jungle Fowl dance. My mother was incredibly nervous but all my Muningawus had told her to get up and dance for her daughter. The women were looking at me as they sang and danced, and I had never felt so whole as a person. I had never yearned for this sense of belonging before. Now that my family and community on the Tiwi Islands had shown me this, I finally realised what I had been missing. I couldn't take my eyes off Ursula as Daffy when she was pulled up to join the dance. Watching her mirrored the feeling I had. Of coming home.

In the same way *Four Weddings and a Funeral* ended with all the photos, Murray took candid snaps of us celebrating at the reception to be used at the end of our film. Naturally, we all got very silly for the camera. The sun was setting, so he didn't have a lot of time before the light disappeared. We had about five minutes to get all of that right, so Wayne was shouting like a football coach telling us where to look.

Before I knew it, the wedding was over. Everyone was being whisked away and put on a ferry or a plane to Darwin. I have to admit I was a tiny bit jealous that the rest of the cast got to go and party back on the mainland, but it was a small price to pay when I was turning a dream into a reality.

I was in the last scene of the day with Huw and Ursula. Lauren's parents, after days of being apart, finally settled whatever differences they had for their daughter's big day. Seeing Lauren as a bride just confirmed for them that they could close whatever distance was between them. They then turn around and see her all dressed up in Tiwi glory—the tapalingini and the pamijini resplendent—just like the women of the choir had suggested. It was my turn for the cameras to be on me in the dress. My parents and Aunty were watching on the monitor next to Wayne. Aunty Maur cried again.

Because of the whirlwind it had been on Wurrumiyanga, I hadn't had a moment to do anything that wasn't connected to the film. But suddenly I had a day off. I managed to find time to buy some art. I went to Bima Wear with some of the ladies from the costume department. They were incredibly sweet, and gave me a gift of earrings with the Aboriginal flag in the shape of a heart. I felt so embraced by everyone on that island.

One of the very special moments for me in the film was when Lauren's mother, Daffy, is welcomed back home, and it was captured beautifully. Because I had witnessed Bernard's greatness two months earlier, I was keen to see Ursula's reaction as he performed again for her. I get goosebumps when I think about the two of them embracing for the first time in so many years. I thought it was important for Lauren to not cry in the scene, to keep my emotions understated and absorb what was happening. I hadn't grown up with this community, so the looks of wonder I gave are entirely real.

Ursula was captivating. It was such a delicate and difficult scene to perform. Her character hadn't really been present in the story up until then but she had been talked about and the audience has anticipated meeting her from the beginning. The audience has such a short time to get a true sense of who Daffy is and that all relied on Ursula.

One of the big concerns during the making of the film was whether an audience was going to be able to feel sympathy for a woman who has abandoned her husband and daughter right before her daughter's wedding. But Ursula took this in her stride. She brought so much humanity to the character. From the moment you first see her, you immediately understood her longing for home and family. You understood her search for purpose and the guilt she carried for being away from home. She was fully realised and human.

Poor Bernard hadn't been feeling well in the days leading up to the shoot but he overcame it to deliver a stunning performance. You would think he'd been acting his whole life! Just as he'd done with Libby, he had taken Ursula's face in his hands and he was incredibly tactile and delicate. He perfectly matched Ursula's stunning performance. There was a little bit of magic in the room that day and I think we all felt it. The warmth and generosity between them was so enthralling that I forgot where I was and what I was supposed to be doing.

This was such an important scene to nail. It's the biggest question the audience has at that point of the film. Why has

Lauren's mum run away? Why is it so important to find her mum? The wedding isn't enough. The film had to be about something bigger. Weddings themselves are never just about the bride and groom. They're also about the family. Ursula's and Bernard's performances made the family feel real.

Next, we had to shoot the scene between Lauren and Daffy. It's the first time they're alone together and really get to talk, mother and daughter. For me, it felt like something was coming full circle. Ursula was there for the beginning of my journey as an actor. I was only on this path because she put me forward for the role of *Yibiyung* at Belvoir St Theatre, after all. She had been a big sister to me since day one, always looking out for me. The kindness and empathy that she carries made me realise that there was no one else who could have played Daffy.

Naturally, I am still very intimidated acting in front of this talented veteran. Ursula is at that point in her career where everything seems to come naturally to her. I cannot wait to get to that stage. It seems incredibly liberating. But also, as angry as Lauren was with her mother, we are also at the point in the film where she and Ned have broken up. She has lost her belief in that relationship. She is angry at her mother but she is also hurting and she needs her mother badly.

As we finished, Wayne was jumping up and down excitedly behind the monitor. 'Yes, that's great, Mizzy!' he said. 'Now, go and do it again one more time.'

Then all of a sudden the last scene was done and we were ready to move on. Tiwi had spoiled us. I felt so embraced and cared for, and I hope the community felt that our film honoured and respected them. I was so glad that I had done all of the extra worrying and stressing in the years leading up to these few days. That worrying had turned into something productive and set the groundwork to make sure we had done everything we could to ensure this film would be a fun experience for the community and positive for them in the long run.

Living away from the Territory means that I don't get to be in constant connection with language and culture, but I like to think that creating this film was my way of keeping something alive within me that I will carry always.

CHAPTER THIRTEEN

IT'S A WRAP

I T WAS SUCH AN EMOTIONAL FEW DAYS ON TIWI BUT IT
had invigorated me and I was looking forward to hitting
the road again. Next stop, Kakadu, to shoot the beginning of
the adventure. This is the part where Lauren and Ned get to
have some fun along their journey. At this stage Lauren is a bit
hesitant to look for her mother and would rather postpone the
wedding but Ned isn't having that, so they go on the hunt.

The thing I have trouble with, in a lot of American romantic
comedies in particular, is that the men can have a very low
tolerance for a woman's decisiveness—it's as if her self-
assurance is a direct threat to his masculinity. We wanted to

subvert that in *Top End Wedding*. So, even in Lauren's state of grumpy hungover worry, Ned stays cool, calm and collected. He's there for the hard times, not just the fun times.

Travelling with Gwilym and the crew was fabulous. One of the many stops we made along the Arnhem Highway was at a visitors' centre called Window on the Wetlands, where we pulled over to shoot on Limilngan-Wulna country. We had a drone following our car as we drove to capture the incredible backdrop of floodplains. It was very green at the time, thanks to the monsoonal rain that had fallen in the lead-up to the shoot. This was the Territory at its most lush and beautiful.

At one point, we had pulled over on the side of the road to shoot some buffalo. With the camera, that is. Still, the poor things all huddled together and looked up at the drone fearfully it seemed to me. They were making little noises, as if having a conversation to figure out what this little buzzing thing around their heads might be. I guess we were the talk of the town everywhere.

As we arrived in Kakadu, my Aunty Yvonne's sister, Aunty Annie welcomed us to country. She didn't hold anything back as she pointed me out in the crowd and announced, 'That's my niece!' Not too subtle, Aunty.

Even though Jabiru had changed quite significantly since I was a kid, I was still touched to be back on the streets where I'd grown up and gone to school.

Plus, did I mention we had a helicopter? One valuable thing I've learned is that you've got to put the damn thing you want in the script first and then see what happens. I'm sure the producers wanted to kill Josh and me: we had a dog in the story; we were going to some of the most remote locations in the country; we had to book a barge to take equipment to an island; and now we were asking for a helicopter. But, hey, it was all going to be worth it!

To the team's credit, they got the helicopter, and soon Gwilym and I were in front of it as Lauren and Ned, interrogating a man—the French helicopter pilot, whom they suspected was her mother's lover—about her whereabouts. The actor playing the pilot, Julian Garner, had lived in France and spoke the language fluently, so his accent was spot on. His character took himself incredibly seriously, and that just made everything more entertaining. Julian's performance (particularly mouthing a not-too-kind phrase to Lauren and Ned) gets one of the best laughs of the film every time we show it.

One of the greatest honours of this journey was when we were formally invited to shoot out at a place called Hawk

Dreaming. It is a very special and sacred place, and tourists are restricted. The fact that we were offered this opportunity is an incredible privilege that was not lost on any of us.

We were in stone country, now. We had left all of the aqua-blue coastline, and were surrounded by ancient limestone rock formations and incredible floodplains that stretched as far as the eye could see. It was the biggest honour to film at Hawk Dreaming and First Rock in Kakadu. Tourists do not come to these sites as you can only visit if you are formally invited by the Traditional Owners, and rightly so. Sometimes only nice people should have nice things. Sean Neidjie, grandson of 'the Kakadu Man' Big Bill Neidjie, had looked after us out there with two other Traditional Owners. They knew how to look after us on country.

It had been a beautiful dry season morning, with clear blue skies and soft breezes. The sky had been so clear that you could see the Whistling Kites soaring above us—just like Josh had written in the script.

There was some preventative burning-off happening while we were shooting, with low fires all around. Once again, our director of photography Murray Lui's brilliance shone through. He had noticed that the light had turned the sun into a spotlight, so we stopped the car under it. Again, the Territory itself took the starring role in the film.

I felt at home being back in Jabiru, mostly because I still have family there. When I was seven years old my Aunty Kia brought my cousins—Joseph, Kadeem and Melinda—to Jabiru. Before they came I had been missing all my cousins in Darwin and, with their arrival, I didn't feel quite so alone. They would often spend school holidays at my house, and if we got a bit too rowdy inside my mum would take us out swimming at either Jim Jim Falls or Gunlom to wear us out. (Crocodile numbers have quadrupled since 1997, so Jim Jim Falls is now closed off but Gunlom is practically a natural infinity pool at the top of a rock. No crocs there.)

Everywhere I turned in Jabiru I had memories flooding back. The local shops where I would ride my bike with my parents. The local council office where Dad worked—and where I did my homework when Mum was away studying part time at Curtin University. The Monte Carlos and Iced VoVos I'd steal from the staff kitchen. The library I spent time reading in when I got bored in his office. My first ever school where I had made many friends, particularly May and Alicia. Houses I visited for birthday parties and sleepovers. Even though the town had changed significantly since the miners no longer needed to live there (they were now flown in and out between the Ranger mine and Darwin), a part of me hoped that the film would evoke the same nostalgia for my old classmates and their parents.

Aunty Kia and Uncle Ian still live in the town, so it was wonderful to catch up with the rest of the family too. Joseph and Kadeem are now park rangers in Kakadu and they were overseeing the shoot on Mirarr Land, which meant I got to share our filming experience with them. And we all went to school with their co-worker Savannah Eccles, who runs a great information session for tourists who visit Kakadu. I could see they were a little excited about the film crew arriving there.

It's always lovely to see my cousins take such pride in their roles in conserving the park. While they don't claim to be Mirarr themselves, the knowledge that has been passed on from the Traditional Owners isn't something they take for granted. It's something they've grown up with around them, as I did.

On our day off, I took the crew fishing on the East Alligator river. Don't worry, it's just a name. There are no alligators there. Hundreds of crocodiles, though. The paths around the river can get pretty treacherous, and at the time we were filming, there were three different cars tipped over in the lake, abandoned by people who had underestimated the current.

You'd think a Territory girl would be great at fishing, but I'm just not. Try as I might, I always end up snagging my line and getting really excited thinking I've caught something— only to reel in a bit of twig and seaweed. The only victory I've ever had with fishing was when I went camping with my family in Arnhem Land. I have to admit, I had a pretty big advantage: the water was so clear we could see where the fish were hiding and I knew exactly where to drop the bait.

But the crew told me it's not about catching the fish, it's about the meditative state of relaxation you go into while fishing. It's less about catching a fish and more about being still. That's good for me because I sure wasn't catching anything anyway!

The next day it was time to take Gwilym to Ubirr lookout, which was just down the road. It was incredible to see this land anew through his eyes. I remember the moment we ascended the rock and he got his first look over the floodplains. He was struck with this look of awe and wonder. He said he had never before been in a place where he felt like the last man on earth. There's just so much space out there. I could only imagine what it was like for him as someone from London, where everyone lives right on top of each other. I think it's really important for everyone who lives in a big city to go out and sit in nature at least once. To experience the vastness of our world is so important to allow you to take stock of your life and put your problems in perspective. When you escape the noise and distractions you can really appreciate where you've been and where you're going to go. That's where I find my happiness.

We also had the honour of witnessing Ursula as Daffy singing 'Muli Muli La' on the top of Nawurlandja in Kakadu. For people who don't know Ursula, she has the most soulful voice you will ever hear. I remember being blown away when I saw her play Julie in the stage show of *The Sapphires* before it became a film. Whenever Ursula sings, it is from a precious, vulnerable place. It inspires me to do the same with acting. It's no surprise that this moment became the point in the film where audiences truly understood this Aboriginal woman's longing for her home and for family.

We moved on to Katherine so rapidly my head was spinning. I could hardly believe it—we had waited so long for this to come together and now, when I had finally accepted that it was really happening, it was about to end!

Gwil and I drove down with two wonderful crew members: Renate from costume and Jen from make-up. I basically wanted to have my own version of *Carpool Karaoke* on the drive, so I made a playlist of Whitney, Chaka Khan, Prince,

Cher and of course a whole heap of tragic seventies and eighties pop and glam rock. (I avoided Queen, in case Gwil needed a bit of a break after listening to all their songs for the past eighteen months.) If acting doesn't work out for me, I'm going to start my own Love Song Dedications station. I probably should have thought of what the others might have preferred to listen to, but I clearly had learned nothing since my friends mocked me mercilessly for my middle-aged-White-woman taste in music. Yep, these guys met Cheryl.

Thankfully, Renate, Jen and Gwil *loved* the playlist I made. Gwil yelled 'What a tune!' whenever they joined in on the singing, and they really didn't have any other option, so I'm glad they saw some sense.

I was happy to be on Jawoyn country. I have so many great memories of being there with my parents for school holidays, and going on school camp.

In true Wayne Blair director's fashion, we had scheduled to stop and shoot at certain places along the highway, for the montage of Lauren and Ned looking for Daffy. It was wonderful to see the Jawoyn rangers come onto set. Like my cousins in Kakadu, they take great pride in their work at Nitmiluk National Park. But being a ranger in a remote area can be demanding, and it was incredibly sad to find out on our first day of shooting that someone on holiday in the gorge had gone into cardiac arrest and died while on the tour. Ambulance and police had turned up, so the poor tourists and guides had a lot to process and deal with. Out of respect to all, we decided to move the shoot. Filming humorous scenes where someone had just died just didn't feel right.

We were about to film Nikita Waldron and Taylor Wiese, who were playing a young American couple Daffy meets on her travels. These two actors really nailed that Californian surfer vibe Josh and I had put on the page. To Lauren's shock their characters, Xanthe and Alex, were sharing a spliff with Daffy when the police caught them. These two managed to take off without any consequence while Daffy was taken to the station by Lauren's cousin, Braydon. As much as Lauren despised these tourists, her anger is directed at her cousin.

The wonderful Shaka Cook was playing Braydon, and he dove into the role. He's a cheeky bugger at the best of times, which made him perfect. His presence brought a warm vibe that helped fill out the world Lauren and Ned were travelling through. It was remarkable how quickly he felt like a younger brother to Lauren. He hated being told off and was a bit of a shit-stirrer but he was so charming it was impossible to get too angry with him.

The next day was the big shoot at the gorge. We had woken up at a ridiculous hour—3.30am for a 4am start—and the gorge was pitch black and so, so cold. That's the thing people don't know about the gorge until they visit: it acts as either an icebox or a furnace, and never in between. I hadn't thought to bring a jumper to the Northern Territory—because it's the tropics and because I'm not mad—but fortunately I was able to borrow one as we headed onto the ferry up the gorge, or else I would have frozen.

I had never bothered to wake up early enough to go on a sunrise cruise before and now I saw what I had been missing out on. I was enchanted by the sight of the sky changing colour before my eyes, from a rich purple to a thick orange then a perfect blue. It was like walking through a painting.

The reason we had to start so early was that by the middle of the day the light becomes incredibly harsh. Getting up for the sunrise allowed Murray to capture that really beautiful light and stop us all from looking bleached out. That was another wonderful thing about working with Murray: he has such a depth of knowledge of how all these things work. He pointed to the escarpment and showed me how the light was bouncing off the rock. He asked me to face a certain way so that the light travelling through the gorge could then be used to light me. The Territory really was part of the crew.

I've always been in awe of people like Murray Lui and Warwick Thornton for the way they can read the environment they're in and use it in their art. Their ability to bend and use the natural light is unlike anything else. Black filmmaking for the win!

This was the moment in the film where Ned makes breakfast for Lauren. The scene is not just about Ned being romantic, it's him trying to find a new sense of purpose. His work in the law isn't giving him the same contentment and ambition it gives Lauren, but he enjoys cooking, and he loves his life with Lauren. With all the bickering they have done while searching for Daffy, it is nice to remind the audience that they do in fact care for one another and are right for each other—so the viewers will still want to see them married.

I should add that, on that very day, James was sending me texts from Melbourne asking what should be on the menu for our own wedding guests. Our wedding day was getting closer and I had left him to do a lot of the preparation because my focus was on the film. I missed James a lot and it sucked not only being in different time zones but also having intermittent or bad reception on my end, and I was really grateful that he was doing the heavy lifting for our big day.

Back on the set, I had some lengthy dialogue about Lauren longing to know her family and not knowing why her mum wouldn't share that part of herself with her daughter. I was struggling to connect the dots, when Gwilym said to me, 'You've been doing so much, you should be proud of yourself.' I was strengthened by his kind words, and all of a sudden the lines came back to me.

For our next stop, Murray, Wayne, Rick our focus puller and I were taken by the Jawoyn rangers further down the gorge to show it off in all its glory. We wanted a shot of me standing at the bow of the boat, looking with wonder at the escarpment around me. That didn't take a lot of acting. Still, once I was there, I couldn't help myself. While we were changing lenses I bullied Wayne into filming me singing 'My Heart Will Go On'. I wasn't hoping for the same fate as Leo, but when you're on the bow of a ship, you don't really have a choice but to belt out a bit of Céline.

The scenes within the gorge were the most frantic and daunting part of the shoot, but we knew that when we saw that beauty on the screen it would all be worth it. We finished the last few shots, packed ourselves up and headed back to Darwin to finish the film.

Before I knew it, it was Gwilym's last day. He, Huw and I (along with the superstar dog Fly) were shooting around the streets of Fannie Bay, following the scenes of Lauren's dad picking up Lauren and Ned from the airport. We played The Angels' 'Am I Ever Gonna See Your Face Again?' in the car and taught Gwilym the traditional Aussie reply ... You know the one.

We decided to finish the filming by dancing in the truck to Tom Jones's 'She's a Lady'. Then Gwilym played another Welsh song, in Welsh, and showed pictures of his gorgeous nieces wearing Bima Wear clothing he had sent over to England. It was a perfect day, but then Gwil had to go straight to the airport right after filming ended for him, so it became a bit rushed and abrupt. I can only imagine after six weeks of being on the other side of the world, I would be keen to go home, too. He wanted to take home some of the famous Green Ant Gin, so we made sure that was taken care of. I started to feel stupid about being sad to say goodbye to this kind and funny man. To me, he was vastly more professional, and was lovely and cordial to the people he had such a wonderful time with.

When the first AD Richard yelled out. 'Okay, that's a wrap on Mr Gwilym Lee!' we all cheered and he gave everyone a hug. I burst into tears. I knew that was it. Gwilym was going to go back to his life and I was going to go back to mine. This big adventure was ending.

This happens to every actor on every production, I think. You build these intense relationships with the people you perform with, and then all of a sudden the show is over and everyone has to move on. It's like the end of the school term every time.

I had hidden myself in the costume truck to have a little cry so I didn't embarrass myself publicly. Gwilym found me and said that he understood why I was upset, that he knew how close this story was to my heart.

'But we did have fun, didn't we?' he asked.

'We did,' I replied.

It's true. We all worked frantically but the whole production was buoyed by an infectious and brilliant sense of humour. The crew, of course, played pranks on one another, often by stealing a toy crocodile owned by Ben, from the art department. The crocodile would be passed around, forced to pose for selfies with the crew as Ben was left screaming, 'Where's my crocodile!?'

It really was the time of my life.

It's fitting that our final scene was shot while the sun set. Trevor was talking to Lauren on the phone from Mindil

Beach, and then, in one perfect moment, the sun dipped below the horizon and Wayne called, 'Cut!'

That was a wrap on *Top End Wedding*. We'd done it ... well, almost.

There was still a long road ahead, with editing and post-production, of course, but leaving that day meant saying goodbye to everyone. We would all go back to the lives we had before the film. I really hope that the experience of making *Top End Wedding* stayed with them all in some way. It will stay with me forever.

After nearly four years of work, going back and forth with Josh, travelling the country, sitting in endless meetings and begging for funding, it was finally time to let it go. This project was no longer mine.

Normally, I treat projects I act in like a sand mandala: you try to make something beautiful and then let it be brushed away. It was wonderful but not meant to last forever, and I knew I had to move on to the next thing. But this film was really, really difficult to move on from. I'd worked so hard on it. I'd pushed for its honesty and authenticity. It had my family in it. It was shot in my home. And it was over.

Now, I'm left with overwhelming gratitude for all of the people who put their faith in my dreams and helped me to achieve them. The people who gave up the weeks with their families to help make this movie a reality. We didn't know how the film would be received—you never can know—and Aboriginal filmmakers are always challenged to prove that their voice is relevant. I felt that I had helped give other people their voice in the film world and, in doing that, I had finally found my own and no one could take that away from me. No matter what happens from this point on, the making of *Top End Wedding* will never truly leave me.

CHAPTER FOURTEEN

NO REST FOR THE WICKED

IF THIS CHAPTER TITLE IS TRUE, THEN I MUST BE *BAD*.

After we had finished filming, and the work for Wayne and the post-production team began, I was offered the role of April in Channel 9's series *Doctor Doctor*. During my *Love Child* days I crossed paths with the sweet and funny cast of *Doctor Doctor*, because we often used the same sets— they would begin pre-production as we were on our way to wrapping up. You probably know the story: a doctor, played by Rodger Corser, returns to his regional hometown, and April becomes the love interest of his brother Matt, played by Ryan Johnson.

It was perfect timing, because the series was mostly being shot in Sydney and James was writing for the ABC's *Gruen*, which was also produced out of Sydney. While it's wonderful that James and I each have our own plans in life, it is really special to be in a relationship where the other person genuinely misses you. But now, we were actually going to be able to spend time together. I remember turning up in the cab after flying back from Darwin and hugging my husband-to-be for the first time in six weeks. Magic!

When I joined the cast of *Doctor Doctor* as an ongoing guest star, everyone made me part of the family. Also, most of the cast had come from regional areas in Australia, so they understood me as a Territory girl. It was lovely to be welcomed into their world after the amazing journey I had just had with *Top End Wedding*. I'm not the only actor who has felt 'post-show blues' after finishing a gig, so I was incredibly grateful that I didn't have time to let those feelings overtake my headspace.

In the midst of all that, my friends Kate McLennan, Kate McCartney and Nakkiah Lui had another surprise. They had written episode eight of the second series of the ABC's *Get Krack!n*. For those of you who have been living under a rock, the two Kates broke the internet with *The Katering Show*, where they played heightened versions of themselves struggling to host a cooking show. They had moved on to create other heightened versions of themselves—'McLennan' and 'McCartney'—as the hosts of the fictional breakfast show *Get Krack!n*. They did a beautiful job satirising these types of programs and the way they can often distract viewers from the things that are actually happening around them.

Their first season of *Get Krack!n* had been an absolute hit. 'Miranda' and 'Nakkiah' had been guests on the first season of *Get Krack!n* talking about their own show *The Blynde Spot*. The Kates told us they loved our dynamic as co-stars, particularly because 'Miranda' always wanted to come across as polite and gracious and 'Nakkiah' did not care about appeasing anyone.

The big hearts of McLennan and McCartney were generous enough to want to centre the final episode of season two around two Aboriginal women. It was a big statement, and they knew our voices needed to be at the helm of the script. So, the two angels asked Nakkiah and me to help them write it. I couldn't, because of the demands of filming, so I am forever grateful to Nakkiah for creating the script with the two Kates. Nakkiah is a source of strength for me. When I read what the three of them had written for me in this episode, I cried. They had managed to capture the frustration and grief that many Aboriginal women like myself have to suppress, and it comes from seeing how willing most people are to have Aboriginal people disappear. Not just from stories, but from society itself. It's as if these three women had looked deep into my soul.

I was still working on *Doctor Doctor* when James finished *Gruen*, so we had returned to Melbourne and I flew back and forth as I finished filming. But *Get Krack!n* was filmed in Melbourne, so when I wrapped *Doctor Doctor* and went straight into *Get Krack!n* I was thankful to spend time with my gorgeous fiancé and have a break from living out of a suitcase.

Nakkiah and I have great chemistry on and off screen, so it was wonderful to bounce off her. She's got great timing, and incredible physical comedy. In the show, Nakkiah and I play two actors (who happen to have the same names as us) who have essentially been written out of a series they were the stars of. The two 'Kates' are heavily pregnant but have been contracted to work until they start crowning. When 'McLennan' goes into labour they are forced to leave 'Nakkiah' and 'Miranda' to host the show.

'Miranda' is of the belief that representation will change hearts and minds, and encourages 'Nakkiah' to get on board. 'Nakkiah' is more aware that the structure was always designed for White people, but has come to the realisation that White people will not come to the table if she is angry about it. They both decide to take the opportunity to host the show, especially as they've now been written out of their own television series *The Blynde Spot*. 'Miranda' is ashed up with lighter make-up and Nakkiah wears spanks previously 'worn by Chris Lilley'. The woman operating the teleprompter has already resorted to prompting 'Miranda' and 'Nakkiah' audibly because she assumes neither of them can read. Despite these micro-aggressions, 'Miranda' tells 'Nakkiah' to 'Smile, and never complain—make eye contact, laugh, remember everyone's name, don't ever ask for anything, say sorry all the time, order cupcakes for the crew so they like you, have a face like a Disney squirrel so as to not appear threatening, be bright, be breezy, don't make a White lady cry, don't mention genocide—definitely don't mention genocide—then maybe—maybe—White people will like you or at least forget that you're Black for a while. Trust me, being nice all the time is really easy and not as exhausting as it sounds or feels.'

But 'Miranda's' rules to survive in their new workplace don't have their intended effect. The two fill-in hosts make a woman cry when she teaches them how to make a mudroom. Another guest, while teaching them how to take stains out of their whites, keeps going on about how great whiteness is, and wants them to support The United White Front at the next election. As the episode continues, 'Miranda' realises just how little the people who make and appear on the show care about women like her. Then when she and 'Nakkiah' are made to interview an all-White panel about whether racism still exists in this country, 'Miranda' finally loses it.

This is the amazing gift that Nakkiah gave me:

THIRTY YEARS OF TRYING TO BE WHO THEY WANT ME TO BE, NAKKIAH, BUT IT'S NEVER GOOD ENOUGH, IS IT? BECAUSE THERE'S JUST SOMETHING ABOUT ME THAT THEY WILL NEVER ACCEPT. WHAT IS IT? IF ONLY I COULD PUT MY LITTLE BLACK FINGER ON IT! I AM JUST WRACKING MY BIG BLACK BRAIN!

THIRTY YEARS OF SMILING AND MAKING BIG EYES AND NOT SHOWING MY ANGER. I'M DONE NOT BEING ANGRY. I AM ANGRY. AND IF YOU DON'T LIKE ME BEING ANGRY, THEN BY ALL MEANS,

AUSTRALIA, TAKE MY FURIOUS BATON AND RUN THIS RACE FOR ME, BECAUSE WE ARE DYING IN INFANCY, WE ARE DYING IN CUSTODY, AND WE ARE DYING DECADES EARLIER THAN YOU, AND YOU SHOULD BE AS ANGRY ABOUT THAT AS I AM! STOP BEING ANGRY AT FAMILIES WHO ARE FLEEING WARZONES OR AT SCHOOLS FOR TEACHING PROPER SEX ED, OR AT ANY OF THE OTHER THINGS THESE BULLSHIT SHOWS TELL YOU TO BE ANGRY ABOUT, JUST SO THEY CAN FILL A TALK BREAK! BE ANGRY AT WHAT IS HAPPENING TO US FOR ME, SO I'M NOT THE ONLY ONE SHOUTING!

I could not believe the energy on set. It was palpable. I was so touched by how the crew and other cast had taken on my character's anger and despair. It was what I had hoped for. For them to see that they had skin in the game. That this society had let down this land's First People and had done nothing to repair the havoc they had wreaked. The sad reality for 'Miranda' and 'Nakkiah', though, is that waiting for the White people around them to develop a conscience does not work, nor does being angry. They will continue to be invisible. When we wrapped, the two Kates came over and held on to us. McCartney said watching the two of us was like watching athletes dominate at the Olympic Games.

I was worried about the inevitable backlash. People often equate the call for equal rights for Aboriginal people with a hatred of all White people; so many miss the point, or just don't care. So, you can imagine my surprise when the episode received an overwhelmingly positive response from Australian viewers.

Alison Whittaker wrote in *The Guardian*:

The crescendo of her anger was vindicating—and these two comic geniuses shifted tone, gaze and expectation exquisitely in a way that shows us how socially committed satire is done. Evelyn Araluen called it 'heart-wrenching destruction'. Tapsell and Lui both deliver verbal strikes at colonisation and the role of TV and its audience in it, which you'll just have to see and wither before.

After that I felt hopeful but I was no longer as naïve as I had been when I made my Logies speech. Change will only come when everyone truly cares about the Aussie cliché, a fair go for all. *All.* Very little progress gets made if we don't work together for equality. So, I hope that when people read our stories, watch our plays, read our books, pay attention to our television shows and listen to experiences outside of their own, they learn, remember and evolve. Most importantly, that they allow Aboriginal and Torres Strait Islander people to speak, and that they listen.

Most non-Indigenous people are very aware of how many deaths there are in the Indigenous community, they are aware of the gap in health and education. Whether they want to do their part (because it is everyone's responsibility) to break that cycle is another thing. I've had it easier than a lot of the Aboriginal kids I went to school with, but I still saw how the education and health system let down my community. I was just a kid, but still, too much of my time was spent going to funerals. Most of my family members pass before the age of sixty. To this day, I still have to say goodbye to loved ones too frequently. I don't pretend to speak on behalf of my community, but I'm aware of the platform I have, so I take the opportunity to be honest about what I see and hear, and I am proud to stand up and create art and performances so non-Indigenous people can see us not as the 'other' but as their equals, even if our perspectives are different.

Top End Wedding is very much part of provoking that response. And it was time for me to see the first cut. I was so pleased when I found out that Chris Plummer would edit the film. He had edited *Boy*, one of Taika Waititi's earliest films, which Shari had shown me back in 2012 when I was sleeping on her couch during *The Sapphires*, and immediately I found so much that resonated with my own community. Like he would go on to do in the memorable *Jojo Rabbit*, Taika Waititi has mastered a beautiful balance between humour and pathos. *Top End Wedding* had completely lucked out by not only having a talented cinematographer, but also a gifted editor who both understood the comedy and heart of the film.

I remember Josh and I feeling giddy with excitement while we sat with anticipation in the tiny editing room.

I started to cry seeing my family and community on the screen. The movie was everything I hoped it would be, and more. This was going to exist forever now. No matter how much society changes and time moves on, this was going to be a record. I wanted my family to watch this and know how important they are, and I knew this film would remind them of that.

It was then that I knew I had complete autonomy over my career, and the stories I wanted to be a part of. We can either be frightened of what this country has become, or we can start using our art to stop pandering to the idea that we are a British colony. There is so much more to Australia that we can learn from its Aboriginal and Torres Strait Islander people. The overwhelmingly positive response to the *Get Krack!n* episode gave me a lot of hope. I really want to be right about that hope. The Kates—McCartney and McLennan—harnessed the power they have to amplify voices that aren't being listened to; they see it as an opportunity. They didn't fear handing over the series finale to us. They knew they weren't going to lose anything from giving the mic to Nakkiah and me, and I'm sure the imprint the show left on so many viewers has made more non-Indigenous people take a leaf out of the Kates' book. To understand that being a visitor means you trust in the knowledge of Aboriginal and Torres Strait Islander people, especially when we all want to advance the stagnant conversations about a land that is burning.

Now my film *Top End Wedding* has also proven that the public wants to hear this. When I found out it opened at number two in the country on our first weekend—in the wake of the biggest film of all time, *Avengers: Endgame*—I knew we had done something special. To do that with a movie that tries to entertain while exploring an important message is even more incredible. I was proud, excited and even more hopeful. And so I now ask my fellow filmmaking women: what is it that you want to say about our country? Or are you here just for art's sake? Let's make a difference.

CHAPTER FIFTEEN

GOING TO GET MARRIED

T HE DAY HAD FINALLY COME. BY THE END OF THIS blissful summer day, I would be a married woman. It was still sinking in. I was so grateful to all of my dad's side of the family, who had put the Darwin mob up across the Christmas break. People had moved heaven and earth to travel to Wollongong for our wedding. As much as I would have loved to have been married up on Larrakia land, most of our friends wouldn't have been able to afford the flights. Also, the wet season would have killed us all. We chose

Wollongong because a lot of my family live in the area, and James's parents and sister live in the Southern Highlands, which isn't too far away. It felt relatively easier and more affordable for most of our guests to travel to. In the weeks before, I felt that our wedding day would never arrive, that James and I would just be planning for it for the rest of our lives, but finally it was here. I had a few Tapsell relatives who didn't live too far from the venue, and had been very generous to open their doors to the family members who had come from interstate. A lot of Dad's siblings prefer to just be called by their first name, or because there's twelve of them, they have the number in the order they were born. I hadn't mentioned this before because most of them don't mind being called Uncle or Aunty, because they know that's what Mum expects of me. But it's an endearing little quirk. Kieran Tapsell (number 3) put a lot of Darwin relatives up. Linda Tapsell (number 9, mother of Guy and Nicholas) and Martin Gellateley had put James and I up in their home. I was incredibly grateful that everyone did what they could to make things easier for us.

It had been tricky to organise a hen's night around my schedule. Also, my bridesmaids were scattered across the country. May lived out at Ramingining in East Arnhem Land, Alicia was in Adelaide, Shari lived out of a suitcase and Nakkiah practically lived in writers' rooms. I never officially asked Shari to be my maid of honour because I was too worried I would upset the other girls; I forgot that most women are more likely to think they've dodged a bullet, especially if they're busy women like my bridesmaids. But they are also savvy women who had all said to Shari, 'No, *you're* the maid of honour.' I was so thankful that despite everything she had going on, Shari was always there to help me.

So, it was Shari who took on the task and organised a hen's dinner at a gorgeous wine bar. We had bubbly and oysters. Being around these four generous and funny women brought me back into my body again. I have a tendency to retreat into myself when I'm overwhelmed. I overthink on circumstances that may or may not happen. I spend a lot of time dissecting what I have just said or done, worried I have messed up. Taking me out to dinner the night before reminded me that a wedding is supposed to be a joyous celebration. Everyone who has got married will know that planning your big day is terrifying and stressful. People's opinions can distract you from what the day is really about. You're often left questioning whether you've made the right decisions because you just want everyone to be happy.

I wanted the day to mean something to everyone attending because I hope to only do it once.

Being with my girls reminded me that this was another exciting chapter in a very charmed life. These women mean the world to me because they had all turned up at such formative stages of my life. They anchor me because when I am with them I remember that it's the people who love me who will look after me when I'm sick. Not my job!

After dinner, it was a twenty-minute cab ride back to our hotel, and Berlin's 'Take My Breath Away' came on the car stereo—of course we all belted our hearts out. The driver was impressed, and turned on a disco ball that lit up and projected colourful lights around the car. I don't know why the man encouraged these antics but he allowed us to take it to a whole new level of tragic. To make matters worse, deadset bangers like 'It Must Have Been Love', 'Unchained Melody', 'Total Eclipse of the Heart' and 'I Want to Know What Love Is' followed. Everything the middle-aged woman in me adores.

Despite the disco ball, I don't think the driver was quite ready for all the hands on hearts, power pulls and melodramatic facial expressions. The poor man must have had trouble hearing after the sheer volume I sustained inside his vehicle. I wasn't apologetic about knowing *all* the lyrics to *all* the songs, either.

When we got back to the room, we celebrated our feminine glory with masks and bubbly. The night couldn't have finished on a better note: *Father of the Bride Part II* came on local TV.

The next morning when I woke I felt as if I were still dreaming. It just didn't feel real. I saw the girls steaming their dresses, then Tara and Emma, two gorgeous make-up artists I worked with on *Love Child*, arrived to weave their magic. A bright pink-and-white bouquet arrived for me from my beautiful husband-to-be. His card read:

> To Miranda,
>
> If you could marry me today I would consider it a personal favour.
>
> Love you today and always.
>
> Your groom, James x

Reading his words made my heart explode out of my chest. Everything about this felt right. Nerves were still there, of course, because I was aware of the audience we were about to have. But there was no shadow of a doubt that I was doing something that was going to make me happy. I adore this man with every fibre of my being.

May put on some nineties R&B, and Shari and Nakkiah made Bellinis while my hair and make-up were done. The apartment was filled with laughter and excitement and lots of cheeky banter. I'm stronger because of the quick-witted and smart women I surround myself with.

It started to become real when the flowers were delivered. James's nieces were our flower-girls and had arrived in their beautiful blue dresses to pick up their smaller bouquets. Then my mum and dad arrived, and Mum fussed over my dress as I had photos taken with the girls and with them. We practically recreated the movie poster of *Bridesmaids*. I love the actresses in that film, especially Rose Byrne, so I'm proud of the homage we made.

My mother and father looked incredibly glamorous. Mum wore a beautiful dark silver dress and my father wore a dark blue suit with a tie that matched Mum's dress. I know, my parents are bloody adorable. I shared one car with them while the bridesmaids went in the other.

The two cars made it to the venue, and we parked out of sight from the guests until we were ready to arrive in an orderly fashion: first the bridesmaids, then the bride. Problem was, one of the (vintage) wedding cars had completely worn itself out after travelling up a steep road. The drivers managed to fix it, but in all the confusion they drove my car forward first, rather than last so I could make my grand entrance. I told our driver this, so he reversed back, but I saw the devastated look on James's face. Silly man, he should have known me by now.

[James's note: I didn't know the car had broken down. I was still in a mild panic because the microphone system had completely broken down. We'd made a last-second call for everyone speaking at the ceremony to stand outside of the pagoda and project and I was worried that Miranda might hate it. When the car started to reverse out all I remember thinking was, 'Oh, this is about to get very embarrassing.']

As planned, the girls walked down the aisle first, and then I got out of the car with Mum and Dad. It meant the world to me to be arm-in-arm with them both. I felt safe. I must have looked like the biggest dork, because I only had eyes for James. I felt beautiful, but that wasn't what the day was about, because I'm constantly wearing glamorous gowns for work. After all the planning, the talking about it, the negotiating ... we were finally here. Growing up I always believed that in order to be worth something, I needed to be anyone else but myself. I'm used to performing in front of big crowds but I used characters to hide my insecurities. To all of these people, though, I was just Miranda. But this time I didn't need to be anything more or anything less. When I saw James smile, I was everything I needed to be.

I did my best to hide my nerves, because I knew that my parents, bridesmaids and groom were all feeling nervous. Not only that, I didn't want to retreat into myself like I normally do. I wanted to take this in.

Beautiful James was very nervous to speak, so I squeezed his hand to tell him it was okay. It's not that I felt complete, but I just felt … content. We were going to be here for each other through thick and thin, and it was because I had found this person. It was as if everything else would fall into place. James was the calm in the middle of the storm.

I was surprised how many of our friends and family wanted to speak so earnestly about the two of us. I was waiting to be teased mercilessly, but I think my bridesmaids wanted to do what I didn't expect them to do. I was grateful to everyone who spoke that day.

[James's note: I *did* get teased mercilessly.]

TOP END GIRL

The bridesmaids came over to give me a glass of champagne, and to just check in to make sure I wasn't overwhelmed. I probably should have kept the numbers down but I wanted to have a big wedding. I have a big family.

James absolutely went for it in our dance.

[James's note: Okay, I was very, very out of my element here. I'd surprised Miranda a few weeks before the wedding with dance lessons, and next thing I knew we were learning a new routine. Miranda picked up every move the first time she saw it while I struggled to remember which foot was my left one. Turns out they were both left feet. I'd like to think I pulled it off on the night but the number of people who said to me afterwards, 'I could tell you were trying really hard' makes me wonder if I did nail it.]

The train of my wedding gown was, in fact, a skirt—and when Shari pulled it off to reveal a knee-length dress underneath, everyone screamed. James and I danced out to John Legend's 'A Good Night' and everyone cheered and clapped to the beat. Then we pulled everyone up; my friend Josie was the DJ and

260

she managed to get the dance floor pumping. One uncle tried to floss and ended up pulling a muscle and needed to sit down. Another, who normally doesn't like to stay up late, and indeed is known for leaving parties early, said that this should have gone for three more days. What most family members had mentioned to me was that because weddings had been so few and far between, particularly on my mum's side of the family, it was just a joyous occasion to meet up. It was sad to hear about life passing everyone by, but I'm glad we brought so many people together.

When it was time for me to throw the bouquet, my cousin Denay, who is normally shy, began screaming, 'Miranda, throw it to me! *Throw it to me!*' She pushed everyone out of the way as if she were playing football, and of course she jumped up and caught it. It was brilliant to see.

While the wedding isn't an achievement, it brought me a lot of joy. It gave me that step back to appreciate the love I have in my life. It's not that I forget that I have people who love and care for me, but it's nice to take the time to show them what they mean to us. I asked everyone to put their hands up to form an arch so that they could see us off. As we waved them all goodbye, I realised what a damn lucky woman I am.

CHAPTER SIXTEEN

LIGHTNING DOES STRIKE TWICE

WHO ELSE CAN SAY THEY SPENT THEIR HONEYMOON at a renowned film festival like goddamn Sundance? I think this has to be the one thing I can't be humble about.

Wayne and Goalpost had submitted *Top End Wedding* for consideration at the Sundance Film Festival back in September 2018. I secretly hoped the film would end up on American screens as a result of it being accepted into the festival. I was under the impression from the producers Rosemary Blight and Ben Grant that we would hear back pretty promptly because the festival was only four months away.

In the meantime, I had an ADR (automated dialogue replacement) session with Wayne Blair in Port Melbourne. Basically this means that if any external sounds or technical difficulties overlap the dialogue, we go into a post-production studio to re-record the lost lines. I was enthralled to see the film go to the next level, watching it get funnier and more endearing. I was overcome with excitement about Sundance but Wayne warned me not to get my hopes up. Knowing what happened with *The Sapphires* made me dream it was possible, but I think Wayne believed that lightning rarely struck twice and lightning had already electrified *The Sapphires* back in 2012.

Wayne reminded me that the Sundance Institute was looking at thousands of films from all around the world, so having our film chosen to screen there was as likely as winning the lottery. As proud as we were of *Top End Wedding*, there was no promise of it getting in. Wayne also pointed out that despite rom-coms being iconic in the global pop-culture world, the genre is not treated with the same gravitas as drama within the film industry. To put it quite simply, rom-coms are generally the equivalent of junk food. I knew it could be rejected, but I was still excited by the possibility of it winning a place.

Rosemary and Ben had advised everyone of the date when the screening line-up would be announced online. Before I could even look on the day, though, I got an excited text from Josh telling me that we had got in. I didn't believe him. I feverishly checked the website, and there it was: the name of our little film. On the list. I screamed and danced around our bedroom. I may have also jumped on our bed. We were going to goddamn *Sundance*!!!

Once I caught my breath I started dealing with the logistics. Because of my experience with *The Sapphires* I knew it would be a whirlwind, so I thought that before the adventure rocketed off, James and I should have some quality time together in a place that wouldn't involve work. I'd had a wonderful time in Ho Chi Minh City while shooting *The Sapphires*, but I hadn't visited the north of Vietnam, and now I wanted to do that with James. I had fallen in love with the country all over again when I saw the *Kitchen Confidential* episode in which renowned chef (now late) Anthony Bourdain took President Barack Obama to Bun Cha Huong Lien, a restaurant in Hanoi. I am so obsessed with Vietnamese food, particularly pho, that I thought it would be a wonderful place to spend a fortnight, so I booked a holiday/honeymoon. It was hot and fabulous and we had 'The Obama Special' at Bun Cha Huong

Lien: local beer with delicious Bun Cha. My mouth still waters thinking about it. We had so much incredible food, and I may have had a Vietnamese iced coffee (made with condensed milk) every single day. The whole holiday was sweet.

Then it was time to freeze. Sundance was started by actor Robert Redford in Park City, Utah, in 1978, and is held in winter. Park City is like a little Christmas village, with thick snow and lights decorating the streets. I remember when we first arrived I tried to step in waist-deep snow and fell straight through. Silly woman from the tropics had treated it like sand rather than ice. My parents flew over and joined us in Park City, and it was so lovely to see Gwilym again after a year. *Bohemian Rhapsody* had come out a few months before and it was a huge box office success. I thought he was wonderful as Brian May.

I was invited to the Indigenous Filmmakers breakfast, where I was inspired to see so many filmmakers who belonged to an array of Indigenous groups from across North America and around the world. I was in the presence of filmmaking greats: Cliff Curtis, Sterlin Harjo and Blackhorse Lowe, among others, and being there made me feel like I wasn't alone. I was especially touched when a beautiful young woman who was volunteering at the festival recognised me from *The Sapphires*.

I'm so proud to see how far Tony Briggs's film has ventured overseas, especially as it is such a uniquely Australian film.

I was thrilled and nervous about the screening of our film. Doubt was sitting in the back of my mind and I couldn't shake the feeling that perhaps American audiences wouldn't understand our humour. There were a few people back in Australia who were concerned that this story wouldn't be universal, that Lauren's gaze as an Aboriginal wouldn't necessarily resonate with people outside of the community.

I sat between James and my parents, so proud that we could be there to represent the Territory at Sundance. This was different from Cannes; I had a much greater investment in this film. And *Top End Wedding* meant so much to my parents and my family. Maybe because they had cameos. Mum and I held onto each other and cried.

At the end of the film as people cheered and clapped, I realised that our story spoke to them regardless of where they were from. People were just rooting for Lauren and Ned to get married, even if they came from different backgrounds, even if Lauren's perspective was maybe something that was new to them. But we made it accessible; no matter where you live, you understand the themes of family, home and love. I was incredibly proud of us.

I was touched to see that a lot of Maori and Native American filmmakers had come to the screening. One I met afterwards was Heperi Mita. He directed a documentary called *Merata: How Mum Decolonised the Screen*, which followed the life and career of his trailblazing mother Merata Mita, who happened to be the first Maori woman to direct a film in New Zealand. Sadly she had since passed, but Merata left a legacy for the Indigenous filmmakers to follow. Josh Tyler and his wife, Tahli, went to see Heperi's film while I did publicity the next day, and afterwards Josh really pressed me to see the film as soon as I could and assured me that I would really enjoy it. So, James and I took my parents to the next screening—and Josh was right. This film blew me away. Merata said one of the most powerful things I have ever heard: 'One of my primary goals is to decolonise the screen and indigenise a lot of what we see up there.' It was as if the words of this powerful Maori woman had reignited that fire in me. The film is on Netflix, so please don't muck around— do yourself a favour and see the walls this woman tore down. She is an inspiration to any female filmmaker. The biggest thing she managed to do with her films was bring together Indigenous filmmakers from around the world and show the similarities between our struggles with colonisation—even if our cultures are different. As I was watching, I was ashamed that I hadn't known about this trailblazing woman, but I also was infuriated that she wasn't given the same regard as White filmmakers of her generation. I know it's on me to do my homework and research those who have come before me, but I'm also annoyed and disappointed that a lot of Australians would not know who Merata Mita was. I should have also known about Alanis Obomsawin, who was Merata's friend, a trailblazer for Native American cinema. I should know these women. I should have known that I could make the film I wanted to make because of these women.

Afterwards, when Mum and I spoke with Heperi, he said to me, 'I've always wondered what it would be like to watch this film with my mum. I'll never know but I'm so glad you brought yours. This is the film to watch with your mum.'

I went outside the theatre so I wouldn't embarrass myself by crying—and the producer Chelsea Winstanley stopped my mum and me to ask if we would speak on camera about how we felt after seeing the film. I'm in awe of what Chelsea has achieved in her career. As well as producing some of her husband Taika Waititi's films such as *What We Do in the Shadows* and *Jojo Rabbit*, she had done a magnificent job getting *Merata* distributed by Ava DuVernay's company, Array.

I let my mum speak first, and I was touched by her eloquence when she talked about how important it is to use your voice when you are given one. I was amazed this was coming out of the mouth of my very conservative mother, the same woman who told me to keep my head down and not cause any fuss in public spaces. I know she mainly told me this because she was protective, and it was how she had survived, but I appreciated that Merata had encouraged her to think differently. The question went to me, and I just burst into tears like an idiot. I really didn't want it to happen in front of the camera and in front of this talented producer, but there you go.

Sundance and that film will stay with my spirit for the rest of my life. It made me realise not only the stories I want to be a part of, but also of the kind of stories I want to tell.

CHAPTER SEVENTEEN

WHERE DREAMS ARE MADE ...

HOME. IT HAD BEEN A WONDERFUL ROLLERCOASTER of a year and it wasn't slowing down much. I was so grateful for it all, even the housework. James had bought me Whitney Houston's first album on vinyl, and he put it on for me while we were cleaning up the house before I was due for another big stint away. The player wobbled a bit as I vacuumed, and it was really bothering me that the record was making Whitney sound off-key, because I wanted to hear her in all her glory.

I was about to make an appearance on a TV quiz show, followed by rehearsals for an episode of *Play School* and then I had a photo shoot with *InStyle* magazine booked in before I was due to shoot a couple of scenes on Robert Connolly's feature film, *The Dry*, an adaptation of Jane Harper's bestselling novel that was starring Eric Bana as the lead character Aaron Falk. While it felt overwhelming to think about what my next few weeks would be like, I was incredibly excited to work with Eric. He had just shot *Dirty John* on Netflix, and I am a big fan of his work.

But one of the things I was looking forward to the most was going to New York City. I had received a call from my agents telling me the Australian International Screen Forum wanted to hold a screening of *Top End Wedding* at the Lincoln Center for the Performing Arts. Writers, producers and actors in successful TV shows such as *Mystery Road*, *The Letdown* and *Get Krack!n* were also heading over to talk about their process and break down why they make the shows they do. Yes, count me in! I would go with our director Wayne Blair, and I was also excited that my friends Kate McLennan and Kate McCartney would be there to see *Top End Wedding* with us.

So, before everything stepped up a gear I had dedicated my weekend to just staying home and grounding myself before being whisked away by all the wonderful things that were about to occur. Life was good.

Then James came into the lounge room holding his mobile phone. 'Babe, it's your dad,' he said. 'It's pretty important. I think you should sit down.'

The sound of James's low, serious voice made me feel suddenly sick. My heart leaped into my throat when I put his phone to my ear. 'Dad?'

There wasn't any reply, just some sniffles and heavy breathing. I was really scared now. I asked Dad if everything was okay and if Mum was there. All of the horrible things I could possibly think of suddenly flowed through my brain. Then my dad finally told me that my cousin, someone I was close to, had died suddenly.

My cousin was breathtakingly beautiful—tall, slender with gorgeous Naomi Campbell skin like my mum. She was smart, with the voice of an angel. She loved playing guitar and singing country songs. And now she was gone.

My poor mum could barely speak on the phone when my dad put her on. She was incomprehensible through her sobs. If there is anyone who is invested in family, it's my mum. I stayed on the phone and shared her grief, keeping it together, trying to stay strong for her and Dad. Then my mother begged me to come up.

As soon as I got off the phone I called my publicist Jane Negline, who had arranged my whole upcoming schedule. I cried as I told her about this loss, and the predicament I had. I needed to be with Mum and family but I had so many commitments; I didn't know what I could do and how to make it all happen. The horrible thing about show business is that the show always must go on. It doesn't operate like most other workplaces. There isn't maternity, sick or grievance leave. It costs money to replace someone and so there's never a plan in place when life intervenes and that performer has to pull out. While most people understand, it creates pandemonium. A lot of Aboriginal and Torres Strait Islander performers experience so much loss within their family and their community and there isn't a lot of time to process that grief. It's times like these where I feel selfish and heartless. Jane reassured me, and told me that all I needed to think about was getting on the first plane to Darwin.

I normally try to multitask every errand, so naturally my brain was in overdrive as I walked in a daze from room to room, throwing clothes into a suitcase. James, being the incredible husband he is, just reminded me to focus on one thing at a time while he booked my flight for me. It turned out the only flight up to Darwin from Melbourne that day was going via Brisbane. I was grief-stricken and not processing things properly so James looked me dead in the eye and took my hand so that I would absorb the instructions he was about to give me. As the two flights were with different airlines, he explained, I would have to collect my bag at the carousel in Brisbane airport then check in with a different airline. Bless him for letting me know, otherwise I totally would have left my belongings in Queensland. Sadly, our freelance lives meant that James had to stay and work, but he took my face in his hands and made me promise to text him at every point of the trip, then gave me a kiss before he closed the taxi door. I fumbled my way through Tullamarine airport to my gate and texted my parents letting them know what time I would arrive in Darwin.

I was exhausted landing in Brissy. I did everything that James had told me to do but I was losing my patience. I just wanted to be with my mum and dad. I felt completely out of my body; it didn't feel real to me that my cousin was gone. Although I have lost many loved ones before their time, it never gets easier. It happens more often than it should. It's not years apart that I lose someone dear in my community, but months. Sometimes it's only a matter of weeks. It's heartbreaking to not even get a chance to grieve one family member before losing another. My head was trying to grasp the idea that I wasn't going to see her face when I got home.

My parents were at the arrival gate when I landed, and I held onto them both for a very long time. Seeing them reassured me that we were going to get each other through this difficult time. I would have been beside myself if I'd had to stick to my original schedule and hadn't been able to fly up to see them.

We drove out to see my Aunty and my cousin's younger sister. I wished I was seeing them in happier times, but I wouldn't have slept if I hadn't seen them then and there. While I was still overcome with sadness, their embrace made it just that little bit easier for me to start to deal with what we had all lost from our lives.

Most people who know me know I could talk under water. I'm sorry if I've ever kept you from being somewhere, but if I have, it's because I've enjoyed your company. When you grow up around great conversationalists like my family, you're quick to pick up the gift of the gab. In sad times like this, my family make tea and sit around and chat. It's not to say we're making light of the situation, but bringing everyone together with tea and yarns is what gets us through most of the hardships we face.

Out of politeness, I waited until I was invited to speak. This was a time for my Aunty and her daughter to put their grief into words, and for me to listen. It was enough for me to just be there. I'd answer the questions they asked of me, especially since it had been months since I had seen them. I didn't bring up *Top End Wedding* but my Aunty seemed keen to know how it went, so I then told them all the funny things that happened behind the scenes, particularly what our family over on Tiwi had said.

It made my heart full to see my family, even so briefly. But before I knew it, it was time to go.

My parents always wait with me at the airport gate. We have tea or coffee at the airport cafe after we've checked in my massive suitcase. It is always hard to say goodbye, and this time it was even harder. But I realised that with all the work I was doing I now had the funds to fly to Darwin for shorter periods of time. Previously I would hold off, trying to organise ten days out of the year to go up. That way I would have plenty of opportunity to visit family around their plans while actually having the time to unwind and rejuvenate away from the pace of Melbourne as well. My parents have retired now, so they will probably travel down to me more than I go up—but my cousin's passing reminded me to make the effort more often to take a weekend to go up and see family. And to also, when I'm in Sydney, check in and see my family who live there.

As the plane took off I felt a deep sadness. Sydney was the last place I wanted to be. I'd left my heart back home. But time stops for no one in this industry, so I put on my best smile and went back to work. I did the photo shoot for the wonderful *InStyle* magazine, who had so kindly nominated me for their Women of Style Awards. I had my playlist of Whitney Houston, Prince, Chaka Khan, Beyoncé, George Michael and the like to help lift my mood. I wore lots of seventies-esque clothing, and I rocked big curls. If only I woke up like that.

I was able to focus on work, but I was so looking forward to flying home to James when we finished. My flight had been booked much later in the night so that the chances of missing it were slim, but the crew finished in ample time and I was at the airport three hours before boarding. I can't really complain, I had two hours to hide away in a corner of the lounge and cry uncontrollably—it was just what I needed. I called James, and hearing his voice helped, but I just wanted to be home with him. The weeks had finally caught up with me, and after having to keep it all together, I let go. The two hours felt like an eternity.

Finally, I walked through our front door and got to hold James. I didn't want to ever let him go, but before I knew it I was at the airport again.

Even though this was my third time to New York City (yeah, no big deal, guys!) this was the first time I had travelled there alone. All the travelling I had done prior to this meant I knew my shortcomings—I'm often forgetful, I have trouble shutting my brain off when it's time to relax and I have no sense of direction. Anything could have gone wrong. But guess what, guys? I *slayed* flying solo. I gave myself plenty of time to get to the gate, always had my passport and tickets in the same pocket, and had podcasts, audiobooks and melatonin at the ready for some peaceful downtime on the plane.

Who would have thought, when you're left to your own devices you stop thinking about your abilities and just get things done? I finally let myself embrace it all and I couldn't believe it, I was going to be like Cher, dressed all fancy at the Lincoln Center in my *Moonstruck* moment. Did I sing 'That's Amore' while I wandered city streets? Maybe.

I met up with McCartney and McLennan on the first night. Call it jet lag, grief, homesickness or all three, but I was on the verge of joyous tears when I saw them. I also hardly get to see these busy women back home, so I wanted to relish every moment I had with them. I asked them the best place to get coffee (joke—Americans can't make coffee) and then I stumbled across a place called the Morning Star

Diner. There was nothing fancy about the place, but there were lots of people sitting at the tables. I always look for signs like this—if it's a popular place among the locals chances are it's good. There was only a place at the bar, between two women eating breakfast. As I looked at the menu I caught a glimpse of the woman's meal to my left. Out of curiosity I asked her what she'd ordered and she seemed suspicious of me running off with her breakfast. But then the lady on the other side of me asked if I was from England. I told her that I was from Australia, and I was grateful she didn't attempt to mimic my accent like many Americans like to. I'm only going to say this once: I do not speak like Michael Caine or Russell Brand. I'm not Oliver Twist.

This lovely woman's name was Jeannie, and she was in New York visiting friends. When she asked me what brought me to the other side of the world, I told her about *Top End Wedding*. Now, growing up in the place we now call Australia, I learned quickly from the adults not to talk about myself too much. It's seen as bragging. For those readers who grew up elsewhere, 'Good on ya' is only half the encouraging term you think it is; the other half suggests you move the subject away from yourself, or end the conversation altogether. I get that you can't be too full of yourself, but it was refreshing to be in a country where most people you meet embrace what they have put their heart and soul into, and are keen to hear about your passions too.

I was touched by Jeannie's curiosity about Australia, and I told her about the places I grew up and had been to. Then, she blew me away by mentioning that, while she didn't know the full details of the issues the Aboriginal people face, it wasn't dissimilar from the Native American experience. I am normally disappointed if I meet Australians who have the same level of knowledge as Jeannie, but the fact that this non-Indigenous American woman could see the parallels within the two First Nation experiences really impressed me. We spoke about many things for a good hour before I read her body language—she was ready to leave. I went back to my breakfast, wondering if I had spoken too much. She told me that she was heading off to meet her girlfriends, and wished me well on the film's screening and my time here in this incredible city.

When it was time to settle my bill, the waitress told me that Jeannie had already paid for my meal. I was astounded.

'Wait, when?' I asked the waitress.

'She did it on the sly when you were eating,' the waitress replied with a smile. 'That's what people do in this diner. They pay it forward.'

I was deeply moved by this thoughtfulness from one stranger to another. It was lovely to be reminded that doing a nice thing for someone else doesn't have to be a major public service announcement. I know I'll never see this woman again, but I hope Jeannie comes across this book somehow one day so she can see that I want to thank her.

I had a spring in my step walking the New York streets back to the Lincoln Center to see my sis, Kodie Bedford, talk about being on the writing team on *Mystery Road*. The six-part series featuring Aaron Pedersen, among many other incredible actors, was set in the Kimberley, where Kodie is from. As a Djaru woman she was incredibly proud of bringing her gaze into such an exciting script. I was so happy to be on the other side of the world with her.

It's hard to box *Mystery Road* into Western or thriller, but I love that elements of those genres were brought in to a story full of Aboriginal pride. Denzel Washington has painted a wonderful picture of the significance of an African–American director behind an African–American film. He was asked about this when he was interviewed on Ancestral Plane with the cast of *Fences*, the Oscar-nominated film he had directed, and this is what he had to say:

It's not [about] colour, it's [about] culture. Steven Spielberg did *Schindler's List*. Martin Scorsese did *Goodfellas*. Steven Spielberg could direct [a film like] *Goodfellas*. Martin Scorsese probably could have done a good job with *Schindler's List*. But there are cultural differences. I know, you know, we all know what it is when a hot comb hits your hair on a Sunday morning, what it smells like. That's a cultural difference. Not just a colour difference.

These words have really stayed with me. Everyone who wrote on *Mystery Road* did an incredible job, but what really made the story sing was Kodie's strong understanding of going out on country as a kid, and having a grasp of the space out there. I was very proud that people were seeing how different and complex Aboriginal people are.

Then I found Kodie at a screening of *Muriel's Wedding*. The Australian International Screen Forum were celebrating the film's twenty-fifth year. If you haven't seen it—how dare you. I'm joking. I highly recommend it, though. The film's star, Toni Collette, plays the young social outcast Muriel, who is of the live-or-die belief that if she falls in love and gets married to a hot guy, people will finally take her seriously and she'll be able to get the hell out of her picturesque but slow-paced and insular hometown, Porpoise Spit. Despite how ridiculous it sounds, it has many poignant moments about female friendships and the unspoken sadness that many women carry with them in their daily life.

Toni Collette was there for the screening with actor Dan Wyllie, who played her brother in the film. They were both overwhelmed by not only nostalgia, but how much the film continues to be enjoyed in homes back in the country we now call Australia. It made me think about *The Sapphires* and how proud I was to be a part of something that meant so much to so many people. It made me reflect on the career it built for me.

The next day, I went walking. Even though the sun was out, the wind went straight through my bones. But do you think the Territory girl who has moved to Melbourne would have thought to bring her puffer jacket to New York? Of course not, she just assumes everywhere is going to be a sunny thirty degrees. It certainly wasn't that. I had brought my Dangerfield *Mad Men*–esque coats, which looked very glamorous but did nothing to cut out the cold. Even my layers didn't protect me. One day, one day, I will learn how to pack.

It was a brilliant trip, and perhaps the best was yet to come. To help me get ready for the Lincoln Center event, I met a wonderful hair and make-up artist called Kharisma. Back home, I'm lucky if I get a person who understands at least an olive complexion and curly hair. It's not to say that the majority of make-up artists don't know how to do my hair, but Kharisma just *got* my hair and skin straightaway. I didn't have to explain to her how static my hair gets in humid conditions. I didn't have to tell her how desperately ill I can look when I get a shade of foundation that is too light for me. I have to think of these things in the same way a plumber has to think about the fridge magnets and business cards they have to hand out to sell their business. I'd rather not have to, I love not having to put make-up on unless I feel like it but it comes with the job. And Kharisma understood what would be flattering for me in photos.

So, I had perfect hair and make-up to complement a beautiful floor-length Toni Matičevski gown. I had to hold my dress in the front like Cinderella; it was very *Sex and the City*. All ready for the ball, I was whisked away to the screening at the Lincoln Center. I saw Wayne, and while he was tidy, he was … in jeans and a loose shirt. Blokes can get away with things women never can. I could see he was nervous, and then I caught a glimpse of Baz Luhrmann and I felt my nerves kick in too. Wayne and I really wanted everyone to like it. At the time, I decided to be a good friend and not compare Wayne to a dishevelled Ed Sheeran singing on stage alongside a glamorous Beyoncé. But now ... just saying.

Although I was incredibly excited to be in one of my favourite cities, all of a sudden my mind went back to my cousin. I knew that her funeral was on that day, and there were many family and friends who were taking the chance to say goodbye. So, for my own peace as well as hers, I read this out at the screening to honour her:

> I want to dedicate tonight's screening to my beautiful cousin, who passed away suddenly this month. This film celebrates young Aboriginal women like her, who have so much to give to this world. Your happiness is mine.
>
> It is an incredible privilege to share this story on Lenape country. Aboriginal and Torres Strait Islander stories are the heartbeat of the country we now call Australia. I wrote *Top End Wedding* because it is undeniable how embedded it is to that land, and it is time we listen to that country's many songs. This rom-com isn't meant to make you forget all the atrocities that happen to Australia's First People, but remind you why you should be on the front lines for your neighbour.

I sat down next to Kate McCartney and cried. As much as New York City had reinvigorated my creative spirit, I will never, ever forget my cousin. I don't know where she is now, or whether she can hear me, but a part of me wishes she could.

Afterwards, I was so touched by all of the positive reactions to the film. Even though many in the audience had never travelled to the north of Australia, the landscape transported all the Australian expats back to the land they had grown up on. One thing that has never left me from that night was an Australian woman saying to me, 'I forgot where I was for a moment.'

It made me so happy to see people embrace a Black gaze on the country they grew up in.

I had many pictures taken of me in my dress, but unfortunately I hadn't got one of me outside the Lincoln Center fountain or in front of an iconic New York cab. I had to do that! So, I got up early the next day and put on the Toni Matičevski gown. Thankfully, my hair and make-up hadn't been especially elaborate, so I was able to recreate it. *I was doing this.*

We were staying right across the road from the Lincoln Center, which meant I didn't have to walk far in my heels; I am no Carrie Bradshaw when it comes to living in stilettos!

I got a few stares for wearing such a dramatic dress in the middle of the day, but I didn't care. Indeed, it helped me in asking strangers to take photos of me. I got the pics I wanted, including the yellow cabs as a backdrop. It felt a bit weird at the time, but I knew I would regret it later if I didn't just go for it. And now, I have a record of it all. For this Top End girl, it had been a truly amazing trip.

CHAPTER EIGHTEEN

ALWAYS A TOP END GIRL

So that's it! That's my book! I hope you read it after a swim at the beach, in the bath, or with a cup of tea (or a cheeky gin and tonic if it's that time of day).

I just want to give a shout out to the Black sisters who have made writing books their life's work. My perspective isn't the only one. To fully understand how multifaceted the Aboriginal experience is, read books and articles by Anita Heiss, Tara June Winch, Melissa Lucashenko, Evelyn Araluen, Claire G Coleman, Alexis Wright, Alison Whittaker ... the list goes on.

But boy, this whole writing thing ... they're incredible at it, and I am amazed how persistent they are in doing this for a living.

I am incredibly proud of what the cast and crew achieved in *Top End Wedding*. And while it was unbelievably special to take it to Sundance and to screen in New York, nothing will ever beat the pride I experienced when we screened the film all around the country. We had premieres in five states, and a big hometown screening in Darwin. Gwilym came to Australia for the promotional tour and it was wonderful to catch up with him and the rest of the cast and crew. But then, once the promotional tour was over, it was out in the world, and I felt like *Top End Wedding* didn't just belong to us anymore—it belongs to everyone.

When you think about it, making a movie is quite similar to planning a wedding. There's all the organisation and preparation in the lead-up, and it's always stressful managing people's expectations—and then in the blink of an eye, it's finished. And you want people to remember the experience, and feel good about the time they gave up.

As insane as 2018 was for me, the wedding and the film both showed me that there is never a 'right' time in my life for something to fall into place. It was Josh who taught me that I will never have 'all my ducks in a row'—before then, I had a naïve belief that life would just stop for the plans I made for myself. I have come to learn, however, that life is everything you do. Surrounding myself with incredible writers like Josh, Nakkiah and James has inspired me to write the things I want to read and see on stage and screen. I have faith in myself now.

I have been massively fortunate to go from one job to another, which is what most actors dream of. Not only do we need to eat, we just want permission to ply our trade. I wish I could say this book is a manual for how to win at life but, honestly, I just got really good at asking for things. Even my husband laughed at this when we were on holiday in Bali. It was New Year's Eve and we were looking for an ATM. While James chose to meander around the convenience store I simply asked the cashier whether or not they had one. When they told me no I kindly wished them in my broken secondary-school Indonesian a good night. Maybe it's growing up with blunt family members, maybe it's because I'm an only child but James said on exiting, 'Yes, I suppose you can just ask. That feels like cheating, though.'

It was my parents who told me that the worst thing about asking for something is being told no. It doesn't mean being told no doesn't suck. Of course it does. It eats major wang. But whenever I've found my sense of purpose, I manage to deal with setbacks. I couldn't imagine doing anything other than being a storyteller. I couldn't ignore that fire in my belly. This is all I've ever wanted ever since I was thirteen years old. I grew up among some wonderful storytellers in my family. They taught me about the punchline. They taught me that the people who came before me are the reason I see the world the way I do, and the knowledge and beliefs they have passed down are things to treasure.

There are plenty of talented Aboriginal and Torres Strait Islander artists who have blazed the trail for passionate and ambitious people like me, and we shouldn't all have to agree to tell the same story to be made to feel appreciated. Our lived experiences are just as vast and nuanced as the non-Indigenous people who have squatted here. I want my community to have a say in what I'm making because I'm reflecting them.

Learning of the staunch Indigenous filmmakers from around the world has reminded me to be persistent when I have something to say. Will that annoy some people? Who gives a fuck. As I write these words, this country is burning. So, we have to fight for the country we want—it's either that or be burned to death. It was Madeline McGrady who said, 'I was using my camera as a tool against the system. To let my mob know—this is the way they treat us.' Over in Canada it was Alanis Obomswain who said, 'So much history can be lost if no one tells the story—so that's what I do. I tell the stories. This is my way of fighting for global change.' In Aotearoa it was Merata Mita who said, 'The revolution isn't just running out with a gun, it's the arts as well. And if a film I make causes Maori people to feel stronger about themselves, I'm achieving something worthwhile for the revolution.'

Learning of our shared experiences around the world has made me braver. Even though the film industry in Australia still believes that we appeal to a niche market, having taken *Top End Wedding* over to Ute lands where Sundance is held has made me realise how colonisation has affected Indigenous groups around the world and that I'm not making any of this up. I'm not alone.

To make our film, we had to convince a few people that Aboriginality would resonate with non-Indigenous Australians. Some believed that speaking about identity through a rom-com would mean moving away from the genre's spirit of humour and love, instantly making the story a 'downer'. Little did they know that my community have both in droves. It was incredibly satisfying to read in the reviews that everything Josh and I had pushed to keep in the script were the moments that really sang to the critics both internationally and domestically.

During our time at Sundance, Sezin Koehler from the wonderful US blog, *Black Girl Nerds*, wrote: 'Stories about Indigenous peoples do not need to rely on post-colonial trauma, and *Top End Wedding* is the new template for inclusive cross-cultural romantic comedies.'

Back home I bawled when I read what the lovely Bryan Andy wrote in *The Guardian*:

> *Top End Wedding* serves as the perfect vehicle to represent an Australia that is rarely given media coverage. The film demonstrates a yearning for genuine reconciliation. As an audience, we hope that the Aboriginal woman lives happily ever after with the sensitive British lad, despite the trials of history, but we also suspend our disbelief for long enough to imagine an Australia that is no longer indifferent to Aboriginal deaths in custody, the disparity between the health we enjoy (or don't) and the quality of life we're all entitled to.

I knew we had done our job when we had so many people talk about how joyous they felt when they came out of the cinema. I understand how hard it is for many families to make a night of going to the movies, especially with young children, so I was thrilled to see people make an event out of it, in the same way my parents used to when we went to the movies when I was a kid. I love that my cousins in Sydney had got all my relatives together to watch it on the very first day of release. My heart was so full. Aboriginal life was a celebration, and everybody was welcome to join in on it.

I want to take the conversation to our screens and stages, because I know that's where an experience outside your own might suddenly mean something to the people of the dominant culture. People who saw it, appreciated the perspective of the people whose ancestors were here long before this land was forced to become Australia. Everyone who saw it knew that this is what is central to this land's identity. It was so heartwarming to read on social media just how much the film struck a chord with so many people of different backgrounds. Other marginalised groups saw their own families' experiences within the story. The specificity seemed to make it more universal.

It is almost impossible to put into words how thrilled I was with how the film was received by the public. Advanced screenings sold out in Australia, and despite being released at the same time as *Avengers: Endgame*, we were ranked second at the Australian box office, making AU$1.6

million on our first weekend. While David didn't quite slay Goliath, it was amazing to witness the people who had no interest in seeing superheroes at the movies flock to ours. Also in our favour was Mother's Day, as many mums went on dates and family gatherings to the cinema. I remember working on *Doctor Doctor* and our director Geoff Bennett was telling me he couldn't get a ticket at any of the cinemas near him because it had completely sold out. It is incredibly hard to get Australians to see homegrown films, especially out at the cinemas, and yet people were taking their families and friends to see ours. The premieres around the country had been incredibly special. In Adelaide, my friends Alisha and her partner, Bill, had joined my parents and other relatives to come and see the film. Karl Tefler (who had previously welcomed us to country when we shot the film) had mentioned to the crowd that because this was a woman's story it was only fitting that women welcomed me. I was pushed up the front to have the Yellaka Dancers, three young Kaurna women, dance around me. I was lost for words. I felt as if I had been blessed by the Kaurna mob.

Sometimes with all the travelling, writing and learning lines, I can forget to pause and take pride in where my creative decisions have taken me. James is very good at making me stop to take that breath and appreciate what I have done in the past decade. I have to pinch myself sometimes that I get to do this for work. When I read that a friend or family member on social media has posted, 'OMG Monday tomorrow FML where did the weekend go?' I'm suddenly grateful that I've never held on to that level of resentment. I continue to find fulfilment in subverting the negative perceptions of my family and my community through story. While studying at NIDA I convinced myself that I would only ever play the best friend in someone else's story. Once I graduated, nearly all the roles I have played—Yibiyung, Cynthia, Martha, Lauren—were determined, resilient Aboriginal women who each wanted more from their life. It's why young women, especially young Aboriginal women, continue to come up to me and say how much they've loved what I have done.

This isn't to say I have dismantled the structures that continue to oppress Aboriginal and Torres Strait Islanders, because mere representation doesn't do that. Winning the two Logies back in 2015 didn't necessarily open doors for other Black women as I had hoped it would. But it gave me a platform within the mainstream film and television industry in Australia. I don't take it lightly because it doesn't happen for women of colour enough. And it should. It was this platform that helped Josh and me bring *Top End Wedding* to life.

Whenever I question whether I deserved all this opportunity, I ask myself, 'Why *shouldn't* it be me? Why *shouldn't* this Larrakia Tiwi woman have all of this?' I know that any passionate performer would say yes to being given this permission. As dedicated and gifted as they are, we all know that actors such as Toni Collette, Cate Blanchett, Nicole Kidman and Margot Robbie went from being impressive to astonishing because someone gave them a shot. Even if I don't look like them, people have done that for me, so I'm doing exactly as these wonderful women did.

Hearing that *Top End Wedding* was responsible for bringing more visitors to the Top End and that tourism had risen by twelve percent since its release was wonderful. The *NT News* quoted Department of Tourism, Sport and Culture executive, Tony Quarmby, who said the movie was a success before 'even considering bookings made to the NT after watching the film.' Mr Quarmby also said, 'Content integration into popular programming is an effective method to communicate messages which traditional advertising can struggle to achieve.' Props to them for taking the chance. And maybe we've all learned something. Who needs Crocodile Dundee when your audience can have an authentic upbeat film with a cheeky and clever Aboriginal woman who actually grew up there? Who would have known that half their job was done for them when we pointed tourists to the experienced Traditional Owners who know the land more intimately than anyone?

I finally took my real husband over to Wurrumiyanga with my mum, Aunty and niece Aleayah. I was so touched to have people on the ferry come up to me and say that they had travelled up after falling in love with the film. Aleayah was spoiled by the community, who taught her screen-printing and showered her with gifts. A lot of the elders were talking of how tired they were—because since the film, there have been an abundance in Tiwi weddings and they were worn out from all the partying. James was in awe of the place, and couldn't stop picturing how it all would have looked when we were filming there.

I wouldn't have been able to make this film without the help of my community. They are always in the back of my mind when I make creative decisions. I don't always get it right but it's not something I ever want to lose sight of. It's because of them that *Top End Wedding* was nominated for two AACTA nominations: Best Actress and Best Film. We didn't win, but that's not why we made it. We were given this accolade because of the cultural influence it had made in the country. *Top End Wedding* truly sings because of the knowledge and guidance of the Mirarr, Jawoyn, Larrakia and Tiwi. Growing up with these groups across the Territory left me sure of who I was and the woman I would turn out to be. I felt it was time for them to be given back their humanity—and celebrated. We haven't survived because of what was brought over here, but in spite of it.

P.S.

I HOPE YOU HAVE ENJOYED MEETING MY FAMILY, MY magnificent husband and getting to know me a little. Thanks for hanging in there and remember ... good things happen to babes who hustle. So be that babe—chase your dreams and make sure no one ever puts you in a corner!

ACKNOWLEDGEMENTS

Firstly, I have to thank the team at Hachette—Louise Sherwin-Stark, Fiona Hazard, Daniel Pilkington, Anna Egelstaff, Emma Rusher, Rosina Di Marzo, Graeme Jones, Christa Moffitt, Claire di Medici, Pamela Dunne and Brigid Mullane. I was touched that my wonderful (and incredibly understanding!) publisher Vanessa Radnidge approached me in the first place.

I have to thank Josh Tyler. If it wasn't for you I wouldn't have become a writer. Wayne Blair, Goalpost Pictures, Rose Blight, Ben Grant, Kylie Du Fresne, Liam Heyen, Kojo Films, Kate Croser, Edwina Stuart, Sophie Fosdick-McGrath, Glen Condie, Kirsty McGregor, Screen Australia, Penny Smallacombe, Lisa Duff, South Australian Film Corporation, Tourism NT, Tony Quarmby, Monica Tonkin, Universal Pictures Australia and New Zealand, Sandy Don and Lucy Hill—eOne, Films Boutique, Sundance Institute, Bird Runningwater, Parks Australia Rangers and Staff, Gunjeijhmi Aboriginal Corporation,

Kakadu Board of Management, Parks Australia Rangers and Staff, Gunjeijhmi Aboriginal Corporation, Kakadu Board of Management, Mercure Crocodile Hotel, Nitmiluk Tours, Nitmiluk Tours, Catholic Care NT Wurramiyanga, Patakijiyali Museum, Murrupurtiyanuwu Catholic Primary School, Xavier Catholic College, Tiwi Design, Bima Wear, Tiwi Enterprises, Tiwi Islands Regional Council, Tiwi Land Council, Katherine Town Council, The Mirarr, Jawoyn, Tiwi, Kaurna and Larrakia communities to give me something special to write about. Sister Anne Gardiner, Libby Collins, Grace Young, Aunties Yvonne and Annie Margarula, Lisa Mumbin, John Berto, Vicki Burn, Justin O›Brian, Fay Miller, Lauren Moss, Sandra Nelson, Liam Maher, Aunty Lorraine Williams, Alfred Nayinggul, Trissie Bell, Anja Toms, Bessie Coleman, Brett Skinner, Yellow Water Cruises, Jeffery Lee, Joseph May, Kadeem May, Savana Eccles, Johnathan Sanders, Jonathan and Sean Neidjie, Dierdre O'Sullivan, Crystal Whittaker, Leanne Page, Mark Djandjomerr, May Nango, Michael Bangalang, Odin Neidjie, Richard McArthur, James Robertson, Tracy Fairman, Kelton Pell, Gail Evans, The cast and crew of *Top End Wedding*. My acting agency Sue Barnett and Associates and my literary agent Grace Heifetz for the doors they continue to open for me. My publicist Jane Negline for always being in my corner.

My ridiculously wonderful friends and family—especially my parents Barbara and Tony. I'm the luckiest daughter in the world. Last but not least, the handsome, clever and funny James Colley. I love being your Ngipurnayinga.

RESOURCES

Lifeline Australia
13 11 14 for 24/7 crisis support and suicide prevention services
www.lifeline.org.au/

Beyond Blue
1300 224 636 24/7 crisis support and suicide prevention services
www.beyondblue.org.au/get-support/national-help-lines-and-websites

Kids Helpline
1800 551 800
kidshelpline.com.au

MensLine Australia
1300 789 978
mensline.org.au

Suicide Call Back Service
1300 22 46 36
suicidecallbackservice.org.au

Headspace
1800 650 890
headspace.org.au

QLife
1800 184 527
Qlife.org.au

If you would like to find out more about Hachette Australia, our authors, upcoming events and new releases you can visit our website or our social media channels:

hachette.com.au

🅕 HachetteAustralia

🐦 🅞 HachetteAus